MARKET SMARTS

WISE INVESTMENT STRATEGIES FOR TODAY'S UNCERTAIN TIMES

HARRY Z. KLINGER

KEY PORTER·BOOKS

Canadian Cataloguing in Publication Data

Klinger, Harry Z., 1933–
  Market smarts

Includes index.
ISBN 0-919493-58-0

1. Investments. 2. Finance, Personal. I. Title.
HG4527.K58 1985   332.6'78   C85-099211-7

This book is sold with the understanding that neither the author nor the publisher is engaged in providing legal, accounting or banking services. The author and publisher disclaim any liability, loss or risk, personal or otherwise, which may be incurred as a consequence, directly or indirectly by application of any part of this book.

Key Porter Books Limited
70 The Esplanade
Toronto, Ontario
Canada M5E 1R2

Design: Don Fernley
Typesetting: Accutext Ltd.
Printing and Binding: T.H. Best Printing Company Ltd.
Printed and bound in Canada

85 86 87 88   6 5 4 3 2 1

For Aviva, a partner who made this work possible, and my last thirty years prosperous and meaningful.
And to
Mother, a true lady who prepared me for the socio-economic transformation which had just started.

CONTENTS

FOREWORD

Rapid changes in daily and hourly macroeconomic factors may cause detours—or even U-turns—in short-term investment strategies. When I read the proofs of *Market Smarts* in June 1985, however, I was pleased that we had not been overtaken by events between the times of writing and publication.

In fact, developments during the eighteen-month period have given added credence to the "new reason" and confirmed that forecasting cannot rely on patterns of past history being extrapolated or superimposed on prevailing economic models. Today's prosperous, common sense "Little Me" must be an iconoclast, a maverick.

Many dear friends and colleagues on five continents helped formulate and develop the views expressed in this book. I would thank them by name, but confidentiality and etiquette bar me from doing so. Less anonymous but no less deserving of acknowledgment is philosopher André Hudson, a unique loner, whose insights were greatly appreciated. Special thanks go to outstanding currency and gold analyst Rami Mayron and my assistants, Alexandra Fangor and Michèle Castonguay, who helped me to endure the stress of writing and complete the manuscript on time. Pamela Miller and Dave Hudson deserve notable recognition for their advice and editorial input during the preparatory stages, helping me condense three decades of business experience into the *Market Smarts* of 1985.

HZK
Montreal, June 1985

INTRODUCTION:
THE NEW REASON

*"The present is a point just passed ... we live in a Newtonian world of
Einsteinian physics ruled by Frankenstein logic."*
—DAVID RUSSELL

In my first book, *Cabbage Days* (FIN Publications, Montreal,
1980), the average person looked up at his government, won-
dering what brought us to this condition. It was clear then that
an economic jolt was about to happen. Since then, the situation
has worsened. Railways have gone bankrupt or been nationalized because people wanted faster and more efficient means of
transportation. The American automobile industry of today is
following the railway. Much of the steel and copper industry
has withered away. The banking system is walking a greased
tightrope.

The victims of government taxes and of rising and falling markets ruefully attest to the fact that in 1985 we have reached extremes—both high and low—in the stock market, international
trade deficits, oil prices, taxation, government spending and
many other areas. Mismanaged and wasted billions of taxpayers'
dollars have brought about the largest-ever deficits in the United
States, Canada, the United Kingdom and France.

Fifty wars are being fought in the world in 1985. Hundreds of
millions of people in about 150 nations are directly affected by the
perils of these "local" wars. Those who are not in a war zone are
still sitting in the theater, mesmerized by actors who try to continue the performance of tricks which they believe can go on
forever. But the show cannot go on indefinitely.

7

Now the downpour has begun, and Noah is no longer laughed at by his neighbors who scoffed at the strange ark that he built. Some of them have secretly approached him at night inquiring if they could book a passage on the ark, just in case.

In 1985, the doors of the ark are about to be slammed. The great flood is upon us. We do not like to believe that it will last 40 days. We hope that it is only a torrential rain and that floods happen only in fairy tales. Nevertheless, the prudent person still will take shelter.

Everyone still has some freedom to choose his course of action. This book is trying to help each person build his ark as the weakening global economy is being washed away.

This book hopes to shed some light on the economic clouds that surround us: light is the greatest adversary of societies based on Byzantine regulations and under-the-table payoffs. The forces of light created the great Western societies in the first place, which thrived when they followed the sound economic philosophy of acquiring knowledge and putting that knowledge freely to work for maximum uninhibited production.

When shall we see the new economic light and return to the principles on which the free economies of the West were founded? I believe that the time has come. When ordinary people realize that the show of the early 1980s has left them with less money and unfulfilled hopes, they will change ideas suddenly and without notice.

What will bring about the change? The marketplace. Tidal waves of speculative enthusiasm have come and gone, but in the long run a market is governed by fundamentals. Sometimes fundamentals are buried under unrealistic hopes and fears. At such irrational times, markets perpetuate our expectations rather than our dividends. Once all the good news has been consumed, however, the marketplace turns into a revolving door. As fast as the mob enters, the professionals exit and run for cover. The pros know that the majority is never right for long. The purpose of this book is to keep you away from the revolving door. If you have already been swept through it, it is not too late to head for the exit before the entire mob changes direction.

Confidence is the basic financial building block. When it wanes, the herd stampedes, crushing everything in its way. The old system disappears like the ancient dinosaurs. When the herd is guided by the ultimate motivation, self-preservation, there is no force on earth that can stop the shift of power.

Who will survive the perils of the 1980s and make it to the twenty-first century? The survivors will be those who prepare for the future by reminding themselves of the past, those who know that dinosaurs have to disappear. The 1980s have provided adequate evidence that, like the dinosaurs, the huge industrial empires of autos and steel must disappear in the mire of unproductive protectionism. The survivors will be those who are able to understand the obsolescence of protectionism and the fact that free market forces are always the ultimate winners. Protectionism, tariffs and legalized national and international plunder are not working in the 1980s, just as they failed the Romans.

Those who avoid the mindless pursuit of market fashions and realize that what everybody knows is not worth much will survive and, indeed, prosper. Still with us will be those who keep a few simple truths: the majority is rarely right; psychology and not fundamentals rule the markets today; and the higher a market goes, the harder it falls. The winners will be those who have observed that economists grow old waiting for their predictions to come true. There is no way to know, for example, whether the Dow is going to 400 or 4,000, or gold is going to $5,000 or to $50. By a fluke it might go in either direction. The survivors will be the minority who has realized that long-term market cycles have had it. Rather than indulging in investment, they will have turned to trading.

They will have anticipated that in the event of a devaluation of paper money, the earnings will be watered down. Consequently they will keep on changing their trading revenues into real money, mainly raw materials divided between base metals, such as copper and zinc, and precious metals, such as platinum, silver and gold. They will not ignore the value of freeze-dried foods, which can provide for physical survival in the event of a calamity. They know that food values, not prices, will ultimately go up, not down. (A canteen of water in the desert is worth much more than its weight in gold.) They will capitalize on the anxieties of the markets by increasing their risk capital in the gambling pits. Then they will convert their newly acquired wealth into tangible and long-lasting commodities. By remembering the rise and fall of past financial empires, they will invest in real wealth for the future.

Students of history and economic cycles understand that the United States and much of the Western world are in a state of decay. The optimism of the Reagan administration has not changed that. They see the problems brought on by years of dependence on government: huge budget deficits, rule by special-interest groups, currency debasement and ever-increasing taxation and regulation. Those of us who hope to survive must not put too much trust in institutions. We must protect ourselves by acquiring real assets, not pieces of paper, in order to survive to the twenty-first century.

The World of "Everyman"

History provides us with any number of fascinating lessons, one of which is that all empires, no matter how powerful and wealthy at their peak, eventually come to an end. The greatest empires— the Assyrians, the Greeks, the Romans—have all disintegrated. Modern empires illustrate the same cycle of growth and decay: the decline of the colonial empire of Great Britain is one of the most recent examples.

However different, all these empires have had at least one thing in common: leaders who believed that the power of their nation would, against all precedent, go on forever. As empires go, the United States is very young. President Ronald Reagan likes to say that his goal is to keep the United States "number one" in the world. The period of American preeminence, however, has been very brief. The United States had a brilliant beginning and some moments of glory, but its past will not keep it from ruin any more than the achievements of the Greeks and Romans insured their lasting power. When do empires come to an end? The answer is simple: when their philosophy becomes bankrupt.

More than 200 years ago, the founding fathers of the United States pieced together the principles of one of mankind's finest philosophies. From the ashes of oppression, feudalism and rule by aristocracy sprang the most glorious phoenix of freedom in human memory. The idols of statism and blind obedience to government were destroyed. A spark of long-buried creativity was released, and individual effort was encouraged and rewarded.

The result was the greatest explosion of ingenuity and creativity in history. *Homo sapiens* develops and excels best with unlimited competition where ingenuity pays its highest rewards. For 150 years the United States permitted those who pursued a philosophy of individual creativity and freedom to reach higher and higher levels of achievement. Without government regulation, the automobile was manufactured. When that was not fast enough for people who wanted to travel from one place to another, a flying machine was developed. When communicating only by mail became too slow, the telegraph and telephone were invented.

Some 50 years ago, however, the United States abandoned the great principles of its founding fathers. The government allowed a stock market crash to turn into a major economic depression. Instead of continuing to build on its foundation, American leaders started looking for easy Germanic solutions to their problems. As Leonard Peikoff maintains in *The Ominous Parallels*, Germanism has taken over America and much of the Western world. Peikoff sees the United States following a philosophy based on the German metaphysical idealism of Kant and Hegel but perverted into the doctrine that the individual is subordinate to the state.

According to Peikoff this new pseudo-scientific philosophy is based on irrationalism, which denies the mind's capacity to grasp ultimate reality and maintains that the mind can be molded to accept any reality. Peikoff observes, "In the whirling Heraclitean flux which is the pragmatist's universe, there are no absolutes. There are no facts, no fixed laws of logic, no certainty, no objectivity."

This philosophy holds that the mind no longer engages in free thought; instead, it follows a sequence based on action: first, action; second, thought; and third, reality. The mind is plastic and can be shaped to accept whatever is impressed upon it as reality. As described in George Orwell's 1984, modern totalitarian states have added the idea of obedience to this sequence; the ultimate goal of the state is to insure compliance with its dictates by purging people's minds of any individual thought.

This process of decay started in the West some 50 years ago and has been accelerating ever since. Aristotle's logic and dreams were eventually converted into the philosophies that poisoned Germany's great aspirations and turned the teachings of Kant and Hegel into a nightmare. The state gained control of the economy; in so doing it gained control over people's lives.

Today North America, Europe and some of the free economies of the Far East are all in stages of decay or philosophical bankruptcy through protectionism, coercive unions and legalized fleecing of their citizens through taxation. In short, much of the free world's society is about to be consumed by the system it has been trying to protect itself from: the doctrines of collectivism and statism. These forces are gaining momentum daily. The free world empires are in great danger of following their predecessors onto the trash heap of history.

Time is running out. According to the theory of evolution, it took millions of years to land the first billion humans on earth. And then: 100 years (1830 – 1930) to increase to 2 billion, 30 years (1930 – 1960) to 3 billion, 15 years (1960 – 1975) to 4 billion, 12 years (1975 – 1987) to 5 billion (1985 – 1987 estimated) and 11 years (1987 – 1998) to 6 billion (estimated).

12

We all have to adjust to rapidity of population growth. Today 150 babies are born every minute. That is a human time bomb that ticks at a speed of 216,000 per day or about 79 million per year. The population of the globe has more than doubled in the past 50 years. The World Bank has calculated that by the year 2050, 11 billion humans will inhabit the earth.

This population growth is taking place predominantly in the Third World. Europe, the United States, Canada and a handful of other advanced nations already have achieved zero population growth. The pressures of this increasing population can be as destructive for the West as for the countries where the growth is greatest.

On Politicians and Hamburgers

The philosophical decay of the West has come about as governments increasingly have put their immense power into benefiting special-interest groups and discouraging individual effort. The politicians and lobbyists have rewarded each other at the expense of society as a whole. Lobbying is conducted to enable interested parties to work less, produce less and invest less effort for a greater reward. The lobbyists pressure each politician to make sure that those who put him in power will get the full reward for their investment. The politician repays his investors by delivering new regulations and new taxes to further the immediate and selfish needs of his latest benefactors.

An influential and powerful voter whose party is well entrenched soon makes a pilgrimage to the politician to whom yesterday he gave his campaign contribution and his vote. He asks him to introduce legislation to further his own interests. If in the garment industry, he asks for customs barriers against imports from the Far East. If a farmer, he asks for subsidies to enable his produce to compete successfully with subsidized Mexican strawberries or Spanish oranges. If a steel manufacturer, he claims that "we restored the bombed-out steel mills of Japan and Germany just to deliver 20 percent unemployment in Detroit." If an American automaker, he demands higher tariffs against Mercedes-Benz, Toyota and Honda. And his politician will oblige.

Special-interest groups are everywhere, helping to help themselves with taxation changes and government regulations. Colorado University conducted a study that revealed some 40,000 regulations now linked to the hamburger industry. These regulations start with the mating process that produces the calf that provides the meat. They proceed through the grazing and feeding grounds, to veterinary supervision, to the construction of the building in which the meat is cooked and served. The number of rattling typewriters and printing presses involved in the conquest of the hamburger is truly amazing.

Who generated all these regulations? You guessed it: the hamburger people who were already in the fast-food business. Burger kings and princes are making sure that no Cinderellas can muscle their way into the protected feeding grounds they have created for themselves.

Politicians are eager to regulate everything from shirts to hamburgers. Strongly entrenched by lobbying groups in the offices they hold, they are only too keen to enforce "volunteer" banking regulations written by the banks, immigration and minimum wage laws prepared by organized labor and price and tariff controls requested by manufacturers. The ones who lobby most, get the most. Bureaucrats at all levels occupy desks and oak-paneled offices with the sole intention of fulfilling the aspirations of those able to keep their political hides intact.

No wonder millions of dollars are spent by the ambitious to become political appointees for a modest salary of $40, $50 or $80 thousand per annum. When a political appointment is made, the media highlights the great personal sacrifices the appointee endures by foregoing his $500,000 salary for $60,000 as a civil servant. The story goes that he has done so for the good of the people. Rubbish. Lust for power and influence makes these candidates carve themselves into the system. In most cases they give up millions in private life to control the billions of the public extorted through excessive taxation.

"Capital Punishment: The Income Tax" (Jeff Hayes)

In Canada, for example, income tax was introduced as a temporary measure to help finance the First World War. Somehow this measure has proved not so temporary. Today the bureaucracy surrounding taxation and its enforcement has swollen to thousands of parasites. They have taken as much as possible from the productive citizens who have earned it, and given it to those who have lobbied best for the politicians' and bureaucrats' favors.

Political cycles in the Western world repeat themselves every four to eight years, when the "culprits" have to be thrown out. It is always the "bad guys" in power who are responsible for big government. Every new candidate promises that he will weed out big government and slash regulations. He will make both the air and the atmosphere cleaner. He promises joy unconfined from the day he occupies the executive mansion or a legislative seat. No sooner does he form his government, however, than he and his cronies become the "bad guys." The average person discovers that yesterday's bad guys were no worse, and perhaps far better, than today's regulators.

Instant Information

Our economic and political system is in decay because of the special pleaders and politicians, who refuse to recognize a basic fact of life. They overlook the simple, historic rule of economics that in the long run people's standards of living can increase only if the efficiency of production levels increases. Money can retain its value for any length of time only if it is supported by real production: the production of hard goods and essential services.

I am amazed whenever I read or hear that "high technology industries," the "information revolution" or the "booming service economy" will save the world economy. The whole point of high technology is to replace human labor, be it steelworkers with robots, secretaries with word processors or bank tellers with computer terminals. For every job that high technology creates—and it does create excellent jobs for highly trained and intelligent engineers and computer programmers—it eliminates two, three or many more less skilled jobs. Indeed, such elimination of jobs is a major goal of modern industrial technology.

The same is true of the much-heralded "information revolution." It is alleged that providing new information, better information and faster information will somehow be a major pillar of a new, postindustrial economy. We all need good, accurate information; we need it in our jobs and as consumers. I trade commodities, and I need up-to-the-second information on prices and trends. I am interested in events of the day and want my news reports to be fast, accurate and thorough. I enjoy good books and the theater—more information—and want the best available consistent with my interests.

But there is too much information available to me in these fields, not too little. While I welcome, and will indeed purchase and use, improved information systems, I don't believe that they can replace a steel mill or a clothing plant as a creator of real wealth.

The "service economy" also cannot replace the production of real things—homes, airplanes, appliances, clothing, food, automobiles, roads, furniture—as the basis of a sound economy. Litigating lawyers, fiddling accountants, regulation-writing bureaucrats and bailed-out bankers do not, in the final analysis, contribute to a growing economy; they detract from it. The providers of these "services" generate compensation for themselves in the form of money, money that is then used to claim real products, produced by the shrinking real economy.

Today, the entrepreneur of the Far East understands this much better than we do. He is producing real products—steel, cars, clothing, clocks and watches, TVs and radios—more economically and of a higher quality than manufactured in North America. He can compete effectively in high technology and the service economy. Asians have multinational banks, sophisticated legal and accounting firms, insurance companies and, of course, computer firms and engineering skills that equal anything found in Europe or North America. However, the foundation of their economic success remains the production of real goods.

While our society strives to work less and produce less, Pacific rim entrepreneurs know that in the long run these efforts will prove counterproductive. We may not make this discovery until we try to buy steel in exchange for nothing more than a handful of intricately worded regulations.

BANKING

1
ALWAYS ON SUNDAY

"Frankly, dear public, you are being robbed.
This may be put crudely, but at least it is clear."
—CLAUDE-FRÉDÉRIC BASTIAT

All societies have had to decide how to deal with man's urge to steal. And so, thievery has always been subject to punishment. In addition, societies have made distinctions between various forms of theft. In 1750 B.C., Hammurabi, the great Sumerian lawgiver, had already drawn the line between a thief and a highway robber.

The Hebrews, some 2,000 years later in commentaries interpreting the Bible, held that a thief caught while tunneling into someone else's property must repay four times the value of the stolen property. A highway robber, however, practicing his profession by violence and threats, would be punished by having to pay only twice the value of goods he obtained during the robbery.

Why does it "pay" to be a robber rather than a thief? The answer is simple. According to the ancient Hebrews, a thief usually acts by night, fears man and his watchdogs, but is not afraid of God, who can observe him anywhere. A thief, accordingly, considers man superior to God, and his punishment is therefore four times the stolen value. A highway robber equally fears or does not fear man and God. In his eyes man is at least not superior to God. Therefore, he is "rewarded" for being less of a menace to society by paying only double.

For the thief to be punished at all, whether twofold or fourfold, he first has to be caught. The ordinary thief working by himself or

21

with a few of his cohorts can be caught relatively easily by the police. The most dangerous thieves today, however, are not lone gunmen or gangs of burglars, but those very institutions which ordinary people look to for protection. When larceny is practiced on a grand scale, as it is today by governments and banks, no one is safe.

The individual, the "Little Me" of our society, is on his own when it comes to protecting his wealth from being plundered. He cannot depend on the banks, which are in grave danger of collapse because of unsound banking practices, such as almost $1 trillion of international loans that will never be repaid. The individual cannot depend on his government, which is threatened by runaway inflation and mired in deficit spending paid for by ever-increasing taxes. "Little Me" can protect himself in only one way: by accumulating those assets most likely to escape organized plunder by powerful institutions.

Acting like thieves in the night has become routine for banks trying to salvage the crumbling empire of the U.S. dollar. In February 1983, for example, the fourth largest bank in Tennessee, the United American Bank of Knoxville, went under. On the preceding Monday, Tuesday, Wednesday and Thursday, the bank's chairman ran TV and newspaper ads, informing depositors that the bank was sound and they need not worry. He and his board members tried to allay fears of default by hiding behind the Federal Deposit Insurance Corporation (FDIC), which promises that every depositor will be paid at least $100,000 of his money in the event of a bank failure.

But the bank was not sound: late on Friday afternoon, it was a bankrupt business. All banking rollovers start on Sunday, so the bank closed its doors on Friday and depositors had to wait until Monday morning to line up and humbly submit their applications for some of their own money. During the weekend, however, an enormous public relations machine had gone to work. National TV and international news "experts" bought the official promise that by Monday morning the bank would be functioning

22

as usual, although under new management and with new owners. The public relations officers worked hard to conceal the fact that "functioning as usual" was what got the bank into trouble in the first place.

This time the FDIC came through and the crisis passed without a loss to depositors. The FDIC, the comptroller of the currency, and America's central bank (the Fed) also came through in 1984 for the Continental Illinois Bank, a much larger institution. They did so by guaranteeing the obligation of the bank to its lenders, those who had millions of dollars in short-term deposits. In theory, the only liability was that of the FDIC to guarantee accounts up to $100,000. But since virtually all Continental Illinois's deposits were many times that amount, the government felt it had to bail out the institutional holders of that failed bank's liabilities. If several large banks had failed at the same time, however, the story could have ended tragically for the depositors. Yet, even when such a multiple failure occurs, as is inevitable, the banks' public relations experts no doubt will try to convince the public that the responsibility rests with individual bank executives rather than with the system itself.

For a short time, March 1985 looked a lot like 1929 in banking history. The governor of Ohio declared a bank holiday when one of the 70 or so thrift institutions of the state failed. Half a million depositors were left in the cold and the weekend closure extended to nearly two weeks, when state and federal governments defused the Ohio banking crisis. After the first dust settled, the withdrawals of some Ohio depositors were restricted for an indefinite period to $750 per month.

The March banking crisis also ignited the gold market, and the metal moved up nearly $50 in two days. Again temporary placebos were administered, and the public believed that the FDIC, with its $15.4 billion, has the capacity to deal with large banking catastrophes. They had, at least temporarily, forgotten that some $4.5 billion had already been given only months earlier to Continental Illinois. What about the 49 other states? What will they do when a real run on the banks and financial institutions takes place?

Hooked on Illusion

The financial industry seems to move best like a thief in the night, in hidden offices over the weekend, by means of public relations experts and bureaucrats skilled in lying with statistics. It's little wonder, then, that in the 1980s, control of the White House has been entrusted to an actor. Things are so bad that only a make-believe captain has been found to navigate the sinking ship.

During the Great Depression and at the height of the Second World War in Europe, movie and entertainment houses prospered as people wanted to escape the misery of joblessness, rationing and endless worry about the fate of their loved ones. During bad times what people want above all is to kill time and to escape from their current unhappiness.

Ronald Reagan and the majority of America's present political leadership were among the occupants of the cafés and cinemas during the "forget reality" period of the 1930s and 1940s. In the 1980s they were swept into power because they supposedly had the ability to deal with present-day misery. All they have, however, are the remedies of the 1930s: fantasies of a return to a simpler and more prosperous way of life. Real facts are either denied or filed away in paper shredders, because the public wants to believe in the master illusionist who smilingly tells them that a sow's ear is indeed a silk purse. With charts and graphs all is well, spring is here to stay. Only sceptics, as Edgar A. Shouff quipped, "would ask God for his I.D. card."

Are unemployment figures bad? If you add military personnel to the statistics of the employed, you have a rosy picture. The Reagan administration made this change in January 1983.

Is the economic news bad? Did steel mills in 1982 produce at 37 percent of their capacity, the lowest in the history of the United States? Inject billions of newly created dollars into the stock market, and new highs make people feel good. When the stock market plunges, the same public will say, "Who believes in the figures of Wall Street gambling pits?"

Is the U.S. budget deficit nearly four times what was promised during 1979? It's all the fault of previous administrations, the media and Congress. As Joseph Granville observes in his market letter, it smacked of Hoover's "permanent plateau of prosperity" prior to the great crash of 1929.

Comedian Mark Russell recently summed up that concoction called Reaganomics and its wonders: "It is right because it is right; you see I was right." Hermann Göring, Hitler's bartender-turned-Luftwaffe-chief, when facing criticism of the "Hitleromics" of the day, said it even better: "When the Führer wishes, two times two is five."

Appreciating his prize check but having very few kind words for the Reagan administration, the 1982 Nobel Laureate in economics, George Stigler, ridiculed Reaganomics. Other prominent Establishment economists such as John Kenneth Galbraith, Walter Heller, Martin Feldstein and Milton Friedman are becoming more and more critical and caustic in their comments. In not very diplomatic language, they admit that they do not understand the "depth" of the Reagan administration's philosophy. Missing is only the little innocent boy who will tell the world that the emperor is actually wearing no clothes at all.

The Reagan administration made some feeble attempts to cut domestic spending, but it soon gave in to its Democratic opponents and special-interest lobbies. Its record deficits, in excess of $200 billion per year over a period of several years, can be funded only by printing more money and, thus, reigniting inflation. There are limits to the amount of money that can be extracted from the economy by taxation and by borrowing, and these limits have already been reached, if not exceeded.

The Reagan administration also tried to convince the public that a combination of tax cuts and increased military spending would result in a balanced budget. They should have heeded the advice of one-time independent presidential candidate John Anderson, who, when asked how you could balance the budget with tax cuts and spending increases, said, "You do it with mirrors, because it just can't be done." In other words, we really are living in a time of voodoo economics.

Today's reality reminds me of the political commissar who visited a Russian collective farm. The commissar, describing the bright future, raved, "And I see on the horizon, my dear comrades, a Lada for every member of this collective farm, a color TV set and, on the horizon, even meat will be available every day ... in any quantity." The enthusiastic listeners clapped their hands, appreciating the bright news. The speaker was about to leave when asked, "I am excited already because I have been waiting for a secondhand Lada for 12 years. I did not understand, however, comrade, one word. What is the horizon?" The man from the Central Committee did not lose his nerve, and turning to the audience, he asked who could explain the meaning of the word "horizon." The local manager volunteered, "The horizon is a place that whenever you approach it, seems to be farther away than ever."

In Russia they have horizons; in North America we have corners, but the message is the same. The corner is always about to be turned, but that mythical junction, in fact, never appears. Instead of waiting for the horizon to be reached or the corner to be turned, each "Little Me" should do what he can to accumulate something of real value during his workweek before the fatal weekend of institutional bankruptcy arrives. Monday morning, after all, is likely to reach us before we turn the corner or reach the receding horizon.

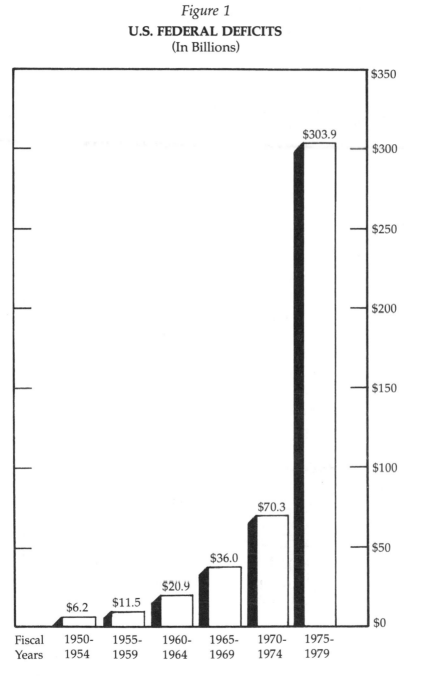

Figure 1
U.S. FEDERAL DEFICITS
(In Billions)

$350

$303.9

$300

$250

$200

$150

$100

$70.3

$50

$36.0

$20.9

$11.5

$6.2

$0

| Fiscal Years | 1950-1954 | 1955-1959 | 1960-1964 | 1965-1969 | 1970-1974 | 1975-1979 |

27

2
THE EURODOLLAR
AND THE COLLAPSE OF
INTERNATIONAL
BANKING

"The inventor tries to meet the demand of a crazy civilization."
—THOMAS ALVA EDISON

In the late 1940s, the new government of China wanted to shelter its dollars from the Americans. It held most of its foreign reserves in a Paris institution known as the Banque Commerciale pour l'Europe du Nord. According to Anthony Sampson's excellent 1982 book, *The Money Lenders*, the Russians were also worried that their dollars could be blocked. They therefore decided to keep all their dollars in the Paris bank and the Moscow Narodny Bank in London. The Paris bank was Soviet-owned; its cable address was 'Eurobank.'

The name "Eurodollar," which was derived from the Paris cable address, was used by *The Times* of London for the first time in 1960.

From a sedate start of Communist-bloc countries' holdings, activity surrounding Eurodollars intensified when American and European banks joined in. It seems that American bankers trusted the U.S. Treasury as little as the Russians did.

Here was an opportunity for the banks to increase their activities, far from the watchful eye of Big Brother and, at the same time, to perform a patriotic service to Washington. What a fabulous idea! The influence of the dollar would be expanded by linking it to some 150 currencies without printing a single note. The rapid growth of the Eurodollar showed how far imagination and American ingenuity could carry an empty scheme. It was a grand performance patterned after the tailor who sold the emperor his new clothes.

On paper, the Eurodollar fabric appears well woven. The industry has mushroomed since its inception by the Russians some 40 years ago. In 1960 there were eight branch offices of American banks operating in Europe with total assets of approximately $3 billion. Today, the number of banks has surpassed 1,500 and the declared assets are about $1 trillion, 500 billion. Just over $1 trillion is in U.S. dollars; the rest is in other major currencies, mainly sterling, Deutsche marks, Swiss francs and Japanese yen.

Eurodollars created a haven, however temporary, for financial corruption and carpetbagging politicians who needed a quick fix after they plundered their treasuries and debounced their domestic currency. The whole world believes that these Eurocurrencies are indeed dollars. In fact, however, they might as well be called "electrodollars": they are just entries programmed into computers. These entries are managed by a "bank" that, in many instances, may be no more than one room, a chair, a desk and a computer terminal. The 1.5 trillion "electrodollars" are as real as the emperor's new clothes. The fact that only "clever" people could see and appreciate the beauty of the new clothes silenced all suspicions that the king was naked. Today I feel like the small boy saying that the emperor was not wearing any clothes at all.

Mystery Currency

Not long ago, I met an old friend, an economist who served as minister for finance of his Third World country for 15 years. We discussed the world economic situation in general, his country in particular and we touched on Eurocurrencies. With tongue in cheek he said, "I must admit that I really do not know what it is all about." I replied that neither did the major banks.

Just in case you doubt this, ask your local or European banker to explain how Eurocurrencies work and what guarantee you have that your money is safe. Ask him the same questions he would ask you if you were applying for a loan: even senior international bankers are unable to explain the fundamentals. The oak doors leading to the private clients' section of a Swiss bank and the uniformed bailiff who ushers you into the paneled office of your account manager are supposed to alleviate all your doubts. The answers, however, may not be so satisfactory:

"Your bank has been recommended to me by Mr. Jones," you might say. "I wish to open an account and immediately invest the $100,000 I have with me." You open your briefcase in a reassuring manner.

Your banker, smiling with satisfaction, replies, "Yes, Mr. Jones has done very well with his investment. Of course, we are experts and it is our responsibility to employ your moneys in the most profitable manner."

"I would like to put my money to the highest possible yield, yet in a safe investment."

"Don't we all, ha ha ha," the banker replies jovially.

"What about investing in Swiss stocks and bonds?" you ask. "Your economy seems to be much sounder than ours, which fluctuates between inflation and recession."

"Impossible. Foreigners are barred from investing in Swiss stock. We have to make sure that we do not go the same way as your country. If we had such an unstable economy, you would have no confidence in our bank."

"Yes, that makes sense. What about investing in gold or silver?"

"Well, the metals have indeed appreciated, but they are very risky and speculative, and gold and silver do not earn interest," the banker replies. "Besides, you saw gold fall from $870 to $300 in two years, and silver from $50 to $5 in the same period. Your best bet is to put your money into Eurodollars. You can invest in lots of $25,000 for one month to one year and earn a great deal more on your money than you would in any other financial instrument. At any time, you can move your funds to the United States under assumed ownership."

Satisfied and reassured, you no doubt follow the banker's advice. Only later will you realize that his little speech has ignored several serious problems with Eurocurrencies. What happens if . . .

The Eurodollar is ten times worse than paper money, because it is a currency with no safety net. You can hold a banknote in your hand; with a computer entry, you have nothing. More than 90 percent of the money supply of the United States is in computer memories, not in bank vaults. Pull the plug on the computer, and there goes your money.

There are more than 1.5 trillion Eurodollars floating around. They are multiplying at a geometric rate and are on a collision course with whatever of real value is left within the United States. It is the largest collection of hollow "money," from laundered drug proceeds to casino skimmings to petrodollars. Moreover, these electrodollars, existing only on bits of magnetic computer tape, will be out of bounds to the United States, so even the vague claim that the largest economy on earth stands behind your dollar will prove false.

The unfortunate truth is that in a crunch, or when a change into new dollars comes, you will have little or no way to claim any of your money. On the day of reckoning, you will learn that the banks specializing in Eurocurrencies have no reserve requirements and are simply out of reserves. The lack of reserve requirements in the Eurodollar market offers a festival to bankers and enables them to traffic in billions of dollars of "money" that are not, and will never be, printed. The bankers claim that at any time they can change Eurodollars for U.S. dollars to be spent in the United States. But it is only a matter of time until a control curtain drops between the domestic printed paper and the naked electrodollar.

The banker who induced you to invest in the Eurocurrency market will defend himself (if you can find him) by saying that all these allegations you are now leveling against him and his bank were not heard when you were offered, and accepted, up to 20 percent in Eurodollar interest at a time when domestically you enjoyed only 10 percent or 12 percent on treasury instruments or collapsed bonds. For some years, no one dared to say that the emperor was naked.

Who Says a Nation Cannot Default?

Not until early 1981 did the U.S. government belatedly make the first moves to attract back home the flourishing offshore Euro-banking industry. Cracks in the structure had become so great that a tidal wave of Eurodollars sweeping the United States was almost inevitable. Spot checks of American banks operating in Europe revealed that, having been given unbridled liberty, they had contravened almost every rule of prudent banking. Some banks had lent 100 percent of their capital to a single borrower, in direct contravention of the American banking law that a bank may not extend more than 10 percent of its capital to one debtor.

In addition, the moneys had been extended to governments or semiautonomous government agencies in Third World countries with very poor credit ratings. As Brazil, Mexico, Nigeria, Argentina, Venezuela, Poland and other insolvent debtors experience grave instability, even the general public is becoming aware of the extent of the crisis. For those who will get hurt in the collapse of the Eurocurrency system are millions of small, ill-informed depositors who trusted the bankers with their savings.

The other problems with the Eurocurrency system might not have proved so serious had the moneys extended by the Eurocurrency network been loaned to reliable recipients. The Arabs and the latest money mandarins, the Japanese, are reluctant to extend loans directly to Third World countries. They prefer the paper of European or American banks to the signature of the governor of the Bank of Zaire. Moreover, these lenders never put all their eggs in one basket. They may extend a loan to Citibank Liechtenstein at very high rates of interest for three years; at the same time they may invest a similar amount in a seven- or thirty-day call loan at Citibank in New York. If Citibank Liechtenstein pleads an inability to pay the Eurodollar loan, the lender would immediately threaten to withdraw the loan from Citibank New York, which could be very painful for the bank.

In contrast to this prudence, Eurodollar lenders have become increasingly committed to investing their funds in the less developed countries. *How about a new capital city, Mr. Minister? Your national stadium is really dilapidated!* A six-lane highway to supply food to starving herdsmen could prove an ideal development scheme. "You live off deposit and interest but we make tons of money off our wits," a Eurodollar operator told an 'ordinary' commercial banker.

Zaire, Turkey, Mexico, Jamaica and Brazil are keen borrowers from the Euromarket. Almost without exception borrowers have debt problems that make it extremely difficult to repay the interest on their loans, let alone the principal. In the case of Zaire, three loans to repay interest had to be extended; and no one in his right senses even talks about repaying principal. During the late shah's reign, Iran had a supposedly sound economy. The Pahlavi Foundation, owned by the late ruler, did most of the over- and under-the-table transactions for Iran. Gullible and greedy American and European bankers flocked to Tehran and delivered good dollars (some of them smuggled into Europe) to an entity that went down the drain with the monarchy.

Jamaica is also bankrupt. Prime Minister Edward Seaga represents a new regime sponsored by the White House. While the American government makes aggressive statements and talks about getting tough with the likes of Libya's Muammar al-Qaddafi, the sub-subsistence level status quo for the Jamaican peasants continues even as Libyan money and Russian interests are building up in that part of the world. Jamaica, which is almost as close to the United States as is Cuba, and the Central American countries that Washington politicians mockingly refer to as banana republics, could well become a bone in the throat of the United States.

Loans to such countries often are unsound, because ex-colonies' unrealistic dreams of instant riches following independence get smashed on the rocks of reality; starvation and high unemployment provide fertile breeding grounds for a Communist takeover. Some of the newly independent countries have the audacity to declare themselves tax havens. Then innocent investors find that their investments are in fact lost money.

If Europeans do not care very much about a Caribbean dictatorship, they do care about Turkey. The Turks know that they are the most strategic gateway to Europe and have shamelessly demanded that their creditors reschedule $15 billion in overdue loans. They have also proposed that the rich nations chip in another $3 billion to pay the interest due. Yet Turkey, under a repressive military regime, is hailed as an economic "success."

Brazil, the largest borrower in history, could not care less. As Celso Ming, one of their leading economists, recently replied, "If I owe a million dollars then I am lost; but if I owe $95 billion, the bankers are lost." Brazil owes over $95 billion to the international banking community.

How could such a situation arise? The answer lies in the lack of controls on offshore banking operations. The success of a banker depends on how fast he can roll over and move funds deposited by his clients. After all, for a banker an asset is a loan extended; a liability is money sitting in his vault. To make sure that the Arabs and cash-laden multinational corporations continue to deposit petrodollars with them at fat interest rates, these twilight-zone American and European bankers have developed a scheme of an unprecedented global magnitude.

Their promise is simple: a higher return on funds than the norms of the marketplace. Operating primarily in offshore tax havens, these banks hide the derived benefits in Liechtenstein Anstalts, numbered Swiss accounts and other tax-evasion refuges. Away from home on a prolonged picnic, the American banks have indulged in imprudent, Machiavellian schemes that authorities would not tolerate onshore.

This is how it works: a few early depositors are paid out of the fat profits. If you are a victim/depositor, you will come back after

THE DEBTORS' CLUB

Country	Situation	(billions of dollars)
Brazil	G D	95
Mexico	G D	90
Argentina	G D	44
S. Korea	L	40
Venezuela	OP G D	34
Poland	L D	27
Indonesia	S OP	25
Philippines	G	25
Turkey	G D	23
Israel	LD	22
India	L	20
Yugoslavia	D	20
Algeria	OP	18
Chile	G D	18
Egypt	L	18
Morocco	S	13
Nigeria	G OP D	13
Colombia	L	12
Malaysia	L	12
Peru	G D	12
Thailand	S	11
Romania	S	10
E. Germany	S	9
Hungary	S	9
Sudan	G L	8
Ecuador	OP D	7
Ivory Coast	G	7
Zaire	G D	6
Tunisia	L	4.5
Czechoslovakia	S	4
Costa Rica	G	4
Uruguay	G D	4
Vietnam	L	4
Bolivia	G D	2.5
Cameroon	L	2.5
Zambia	L D	2.5
Iraq	OP L	2.5

OPEC Member	OP
Long-term Problems	L
Short-term Problems	S
Grave Problems	G
Reschedule	D

some time and actually be paid your high interest. You will brag to your friends about your clever investment, and they will spread the word. You may even be induced to take out a second mortgage on your home at 15 percent in order to invest it in the Eurodollar market at 20 percent. You do not doubt for a moment the creditability of the bank, for it has a big name like "Chase Manhattan," "BankAmerica" or "Citibank" linked to it.

But even the flimsy safety net of the U.S. Federal Reserve System has no jurisdiction over the activities of the Eurodollar market. When Brazil or Zaire officially goes broke (they are broke now, but have not admitted it yet) or the ayatollah is after the hide of your banker, from whom will you claim your assets?

For it appears that, after the banks took their cut off your deposit, they invested some of it in gold straight out of the International Monetary Fund (IMF) auction. They then lent the remaining funds to very poor less-developed countries prepared to pay very high rates of interest. The gentlemen signing on behalf of their country, which is already in financial shambles, could not care less about tomorrow.

When Citicorp or Chase Manhattan finally admits that it will never be repaid, it has to save face and make sure that the balance sheet will not be affected through the elimination of an "asset," such as a loan to Zaire. So it organizes yet another loan to the bankrupt debtor to enable the country to pay the interest. It is like offering a throat lozenge to a tubercular. They seem to have borrowed their motto from Dr. Paul Joseph Goebbels: the bigger the lie, the more credible it is.

Sometimes, when a bank runs short of funds, it contacts another bank that may have a surplus of liabilities (deposits), and a transfer is effected. For example, let us assume that Ancerbank Liechtenstein has requested a loan and International Trust Zurich confirms that $100 million are available for, say, 36 months at 14 percent per annum. These funds may then be loaned by Ancerbank Liechtenstein to a National Development Corporation of a

Third World regime. Its signature ostensibly represents a promise to repay.

Now Ancerbank Liechtenstein has the funds needed by the "Malalongwe National Development Corporation," which has agreed to pay 1 percent above 14 percent —it sounds innocent enough— less 7.5 percent commission. The Malalongwe delegation agrees to sign promissory notes underwritten by their minister of finance to repay $100 million plus interest.

Here is the payoff: the Malalongwe Exploration Corporation receives only $92.5 million. The commission of $7.5 million is divided immediately among the parties involved. The ministerial delegation gets its share (over and above the three nights on the town paid by Ancerbank). The chairman of the National Development Corporation knows very well that he may not hold his position in three years. His benefactor, the president, may be deposed by then. In many instances he will sign the promissory notes with the sure knowledge that his corporation will not be able to repay the loan in 36 years, let alone 36 months. In the meantime, his personal numbered account in Switzerland is boosted by a few more gold bars provided by the present deal.

The World of Masai

The minister of finance has similar sweet dreams. After all, until the first default takes place, who knows what might happen in the world. And besides, he was taught that the white people took all their wealth from the blacks. Therefore, a loan that is not repaid represents only a small repossession of capital that used to belong to his ancestors. This philosophy, which I call the Masai concept, has entrenched itself among most less-developed countries, wherever they are.

The Masai concept has been developed and very successfully implemented by tribes on the shores of Lake Victoria and the borders of Kenya, Tanzania and Uganda. The Masai believe that God gave them all the cattle in the world; therefore, whenever they raid or steal cattle from another tribe, they are merely retrieving part of their own property. When you steal in style, you are not a thief but a warrior and can be proud of your profession.

Third World countries are not the only recipients of questionable loans. If one subscribes to the scenario that the Communist bloc wants to bring about the downfall of Western imperialism through both military and economic measures, it is quite macabre that Communist countries have become substantial borrowers on the Euromarket. Poland heads the list. No one believes that Poland will repay loans of over $30 billion in principal. It will be a minor miracle if the Polish government is able to pay the interest on its mammoth debt to Western banks. If the balance-of-payment situation in that financially beleaguered, plagued country ever improves and a small jar of honey is made available, the Russian bear will surely get the first lick.

(It is rumored that the real troubles in Poland started several months before the 1980 Moscow Olympics, when some railway workers discovered that truckloads of meat, packed in tins labeled as paint, were being sent from Poland to Russia to create a façade of prosperity for the foreigners visiting Moscow for the Games.)

The Beginning of the End

It is unfair to claim that all Eurocurrencies, which include Euromarks and Eurofrancs, are being extended indiscriminately to corrupt and unstable regimes. Some loans are prudent and are being repaid; but enough unsound loans exist to make the situation intolerable. One thing is clear: when a massive failure of debtors takes place, a run on the banks will occur. Depositors with any sense will descend on their banks and demand an immediate refund or more tangible collateral.

The holders of fancy computer electrodollars will seek to convert them into something real, even into depleted paper dollars. A trillion and a half Eurodollars will try to enter the United States or be converted, even in small part, into gold and silver. When this avalanche threatens the American coast, protective controls will be legislated. These may slow the advance but not stop it.

38

How real is such a danger? It is much closer than you may fear. The banks are running out of ignorant depositors. Stripping Peter to dress Paul cannot continue forever, particularly in the wake of an almost universal disenchantment with politicians' promises of combating inflation or fighting recession.

The failure of a bank wheeling and dealing in Eurodollars cannot be compared to the bankruptcy of a manufacturing plant that may have some salvageable assets or machinery that can be sold to repay ten or twenty cents on the dollar. The failure of most Eurocurrency banks is analogous to the relationship between your broker and the stock exchange. When a collapse in certain stocks drags your broker down, all you will see under the auctioneer's gavel are some desks, chairs and office supplies. When a bank goes, the office furnishings will be joined by a downed computer terminal.

The enemies of capitalism could not have wished or hoped for any greater effect from their hedging actions of the 1950s. What started as a sound and harmless Soviet idea turned into a guided missile launched by capitalist financial barons on a destructive course. Reacting to emergencies, the barons have no time to take any action.

The cure, and how things will stack up for the defunct Third World countries, is inextricably linked to gold. Sooner rather than later, the oil caliphs and the other holders of Eurocurrency balances will seek to convert their wealth into gold. They soon will be prepared to pay any price for gold rather than have assets in a soon-to-be defaulted loan to a developing country.

Many Europeans have already learned this lesson. They never have believed in their politicians, who come and go with regularity and produce unwanted wars. Italy has had 30 governments in the last 35 years; France and some others do not lag far behind. The Swiss are petrified that next time the Russians will not stop in Prague but will roll across the Alps; the Germans are terrified that their funds stashed away in Switzerland will disappear. The French, who prudently maintain that "money is not money until it is in Geneva," are convinced that Turkey could be the next Iran. Belgian businessmen have always kept three sets of books: an accurate set for the partners, a second for the taxation authorities and a third to hand over to the commander of the next invading army.

The Europeans learned the uselessness of paper the hard way; time and again they learned that in times of instability, refugees are able to hide very little on their bodies. They know that gold may buy them liberty. When life itself is on the line priorities shift very fast.

The credit bubble is bursting, and so is the fiber holding the Western world together. Politicians, to keep themselves in office, will sacrifice millions of their fellow citizens to fight the next war. The Communist world, which has effortlessly taken over some 30 countries in the past 15 years, ensures through its foreign policy that wars will be of a localized nature; "salami" conquest is still the easiest. Civil wars between militant elements, which emerged in all ex-Western colonies against new corrupt establishments, have erupted. What we used to know as the Western world is changing hourly.

Unfortunately, neither you nor I can stop this disintegration of our society. The time of "Little Me" has arrived. The prudent among us will soon retreat to the bottom line of selfishness, and "What's in it for me?" will prevail until new foundations are laid to replace a rotten and corrupt economic structure. If such an exercise succeeds, it will be a painful, purifying bonfire, fueled by tons of pieces of paper smeared with ink, which politicians want us to believe is money.

3
BANKING
IN SWITZERLAND

"When you see a Swiss banker jump out the window, follow him—
there is certainly money to be made."
—VOLTAIRE

The Swiss are the pioneers of bank secrecy. They have been exporting their banking services all over the world in order to import money and valuables from other countries into Switzerland. Traditionally, the identities of their clients have been protected. Employees of Swiss banks or financial institutions are subject to secrecy regulations; those who release or make use of information are liable to heavy penalties, including jail.

Armed with such deterrents, the Swiss banking community has been able to flourish and move ahead, while in the rest of the world the banking industry is almost in a state of delirium. Recently, a liberal lobby in the Swiss National Assembly proposed relaxing the bank secrecy laws: the proposed legislation was defeated with a 74 percent vote against it in a 1984 referendum.

The thrust of the proposed draft law, which may come back for another vote by the end of this century, is that infringement on secrecy by negligence rather than by design would no longer be a crime. In other words, a bank employee who was suborned by the agent of a non-Swiss government could plead ignorance and go free. Further, it is proposed that incitement to breach confidentiality would be punishable only if confidentiality were in fact breached. (This is like saying attempted murder is only a crime if the murder is successful.)

The laws under attack were introduced in 1934 to enforce

secrecy and bar Swiss bank employees from being compromised by Nazi spies who were trying to locate the holdings of exiled Jews and opponents of the Berlin regime. With only relatively minor scandals, Swiss banking secrecy has worked quite well for more than 50 years. Banking in Switzerland has become a fine art, unequaled in any other country of the world. Some maintain that Swiss banking is the closest you can come to a real religion. Be that as it may, nobody disputes that the Swiss wrote the book on practical banking — sound, private banking.

About a decade ago, the 1934 laws were eased in the wake of charges by various governments that some Swiss banking institutions were a laundering haven for organized crime. They alleged that if the Swiss would only prevent certain individuals or groups from barricading themselves behind "numbered accounts," international terrorism would subside, all taxes owing various governments would be paid, ransom and protection rackets would cease, drug traffic would disappear and misery would vanish from the world.

These demands received little prominence except in newspaper headlines. However, some Swiss banks have succumbed to U.S. Internal Revenue Service pressure and introduced a form to be signed by American passport holders and residents. Once executed, this form absolves the bank from penalties which they would otherwise face in Switzerland if information pertaining to account holders were disclosed to outsiders or to any authority, Swiss or foreign, without a specific Swiss court order. France and Italy, with their weak currencies and weak economies, also are pressuring the Swiss over their traditional secrecy.

American citizens have not been barred effectively from opening accounts in Switzerland, but by doing so they face the possibility of exposure when demanded by U.S. fiscal authorities. The introduction of this special form by some banks in 1974 affected U.S. citizens only, who now face four alternatives: contravene U.S. laws by not reporting an account in Switzerland; declare the existence of the account and thus reduce, if not destroy, the value of any nest egg; explore certain alternatives within Switzerland; or look for alternatives outside Switzerland.

It's important to remember that not all Swiss banks require American clients to execute these "U.S. Forms." The banks that do are large banks, which often have branch offices in the United States; smaller banks use the forms as a way of politely discouraging American business. There are still many sound Swiss banks that will respect the confidentiality of their American clients' records.

As to the newly proposed changes, it would be a fair assumption that the Swiss banking community will show enough strength to impose its will on its government. It stands to reason that depositors in Switzerland will also, in the future, enjoy adequate protection from being exposed to potential harassment by sometimes extreme governments in their country of domicile. Any further relaxation of Swiss secrecy laws will cut into the neutrality and absolute nonalignment that the country of the Alps has been practicing for centuries. The Swiss bankers, who really run the country, will not tolerate any new laws that may emaciate their grip and the hegemony of their banks.

Choosing a Swiss Bank

Before dropping anchor in Switzerland, remember that an account in the country of the Alps should be tailored to your needs and personality. (This book may be less than helpful, for example, for someone wanting to set up money-laundering facilities.) Even if your intentions are diversification and nest egging, consulting an expert to adapt a Swiss bank account to your specific aims could prove invaluable. One word of advice: avoid general solutions and secrets revealed in study tours to Zurich or heavily attended seminars. Your financial home in Switzerland should be as individual as you are.

There are several important points to remember when you open a Swiss bank account. First, choose your banker with care. Make sure that your Swiss banker is a Swiss national who is bound by Swiss banking secrecy and Swiss laws. Even the Swiss banking system is not completely immune. A few years ago, the Special Branch of Scotland Yard infiltrated one of the major Swiss banks and caused a scandal in the banking community.

A prudent American or Canadian will not use an overseas branch of a bank headquartered in his homeland, or even a Swiss bank that has a major presence there. The reasons are very simple. A bank with headquarters in North America or that does profitable business in North America is much less likely to resist political and economic pressures applied by a foreign government. Your Swiss bank should have prudent reserves, be well managed and have no exposure in your country of residence.

When you move money into a Swiss bank account or place cash into a safety deposit box, it has to be done so you will be able to sleep peacefully. What is the sense of opening a Swiss bank account when the records of the investment seminar or newsletter that taught you to do so can be summoned at any moment? Indeed, your tutor may have been an employee of the IRS. Be careful not to leave a paper trail at home.

Those residing in a very strict economy or in a police or dictatorial state may want to take up the Swiss banks' option of leaving the safety deposit box keys with the bank. After using your safety deposit box, you simply return the key to the custodian, who will put it in a small box that will be sealed with wax. You sign on the wax, and the key is then stored in a special vault until your next visit to the bank.

Depositor Beware

Swiss banks do not accept wills or disposal instructions in the event of the death of the account holder. It is advisable, therefore, to designate a beneficiary by giving a power of attorney to a trustworthy spouse or agent that will remain valid after the death of the account holder. All this must, of course, be arranged while the account holder is alive in order to dispose of the account without further formalities at the time of death.

Another possibility is to establish a joint account; each party

44

can have the power to sign singly, even beyond the death of a joint holder. As a rule, there are no estate or death taxes on assets on deposit with a Swiss bank if the deceased was not a resident of Switzerland.

If you wish to conceal the name of your bank and the location of your safety deposit box, all you have to do is deposit the signature of your agent with your will. You may do so by leaving it in the office of a Swiss lawyer or trustee and notifying your spouse or agent that in the event of your death, they should see your Swiss lawyer, who will direct them to your holdings. The point is that you should not reveal any more information than you must. If you want a Swiss bank account, you should get one only after thorough investigation or on reliable recommendation, and you should exercise discretion in its use.

Soon after the infamous U.S. Forms were introduced in Switzerland, industrious individuals outside Switzerland jumped on the financial privacy bankwagon. Tax havens with ostensibly stringent bank secrecy laws popped up around the United States. Some of the Caribbean islands discovered that international banking could be far more lucrative than growing bananas or pineapples. In the last few years, many islands have garnished their official brochures with allegations of stability by highlighting the number of banking institutions that are established and operating on their territory.

Even the Swiss banks had no alternative but to open branches in the Caribbean and Panama. They had to cater to a demand and an ever-increasing competition that endangered the livelihood and good reputation of the old Swiss banking establishment. For international wheeling and dealing, (e.g., inflating or deflating values of export invoices through the creation of offshore "offices"), the islands sometimes prove adequate. In most instances, however, customs officials in the United States or Canada apply careful scrutiny to certificates of origin and value that they suspect may have been doctored in the islands.

The ignorance of some of the promoters of hastily assembled tax and money havens provided an easy target for criticism of half-baked shelters sold en masse from display booths in investment seminars or through the North American press. The lack of expertise in international banking and "offshoring" by many Caribbean islands was well demonstrated during the Carter administration, when companies such as Boeing, Lockheed and Northrup were exposed in bribery scandals. The Swiss just loved it. They maintained smugly, "Anyone trying to do business in such a primitive and dumb way deserves to be caught." And they were right.

The Swiss hold that not even one American firm was compromised, through the so-called Foreign Corrupt Practices Act, while banking in Switzerland. The act labels it a crime for an American corporation to bribe or falsify accounting records to conceal payoffs when promoting sales. The Swiss maintain that banking secrets are esoteric and should remain within expert control, and that anyone who is happy with inferior substitutes should be prepared to face the consequences.

A storm is now brewing in the Caribbean basin. It has received little attention in the American press, but the fact is that the recent Caribbean Economic Initiative proposed by the Reagan administration involved more than noble intentions of helping the islanders stave off leftist takeovers or make ends meet during an economic slump. The aid was contingent on removing from the islands the lucrative income generated by tax schemes for U.S. residents. The confidentiality that American banks in Nassau or the Cayman Islands could offer was always questionable, but even if it existed, it is about to end. Their feeble regimes and almost bankrupt economies will crumble if American tourists are unwilling and unable to finance Nassau casinos. The islands will no doubt give in to American demands for complete disclosure of "secret" banking practices and their depositors' records. The Bahamian government of Prime Minister Lynden Pindling is being destabilized by the CIA and IRS, which have accused him of corruption and caused a domestic investigation that may ruin him.

Today there is almost a consensus that this new assault on Caribbean tax havens is a forerunner of additional exchange control measures that the United States may impose. The new laws are not designed for welfare recipients; rather, they are aimed at middle and upper income Americans who became nervous and frustrated in recent years by the introduction of laws pertaining to personal wealth and money movement liberties. The 1982 and 1984 tax "reform" laws have only made matters worse.

The Swiss are prepared for the demise of offshore Caribbean banking. "Finance is like sex; the majority of people want it in private, not spread on beaches under palm trees," scoffed a Swiss banker living in Nassau when asked about the Bahamian banking system. "There is no system," he told me. "All we have here are typewriters and, for a fee, we splash on paper whatever our valued clients instruct us to serve a dubious or obvious purpose in the country of their domicile. How serious can a Bahamian banking system be, when in all of Nassau you do not have even one decent armored security car to transport valuables? The entire real wealth of these islands can be put into two safety deposit boxes in any suburban Zurich bank." Turning somewhat more serious, he added, "However, even we, a large Swiss bank, maintain an office here, because we cannot let business slip or pass by without having a finger in it. While we look forward to another year or two in the sun, I am sure that fantasy banking has about had it."

Recently, this banker visited Canada and was greatly impressed with the liberties that depositors, both Canadian and non-Canadian, still enjoy. In a typical sarcastic manner he commented, "With such liberties and no restrictions on capital movement, with sophistication and financial knowledge that match those of large money metropolitan areas such as London, New York and Zurich, all you need in Montreal is some sun and a few palm trees, and Switzerland will be in real danger. I do hope that you will not give in to too much intervention from the south."

4
THE BLACK PETER
SYNDROME

"Never before in history has so much been owed by so few to so few."
— (*THE ECONOMIST*)

"Sauve qui peut"
— FRENCH PROVERB

The year was 1973. It was late afternoon in Zurich when the international banker and I had completed the final draft of a loan to a developing country. He was happy, having placed the loan at 1 percent above the London Inter Bank Rate (LIBOR). Over a friendly drink, the conversation touched on the inevitable.

"You maintain," said the banker, "that a dollar without free convertibility into gold is doomed. What are your reasons?"

From my briefcase I produced a pack of playing cards designed for children. The first card facing up pictured a smiling chimney sweep and carried the name "Der Schwarzer Peter," Black Peter.

"Here is your reason," I said. "On the way to Zurich, I asked the flight attendant for a deck of cards to pass the time on the long flight from Africa. She had run out of playing cards and apologetically asked if she could instead offer me some cards for my children.

"Here is your reason," I repeated. "Remember how, as children, our eyes brightened when a victim pulled Black Peter from our fingertips. Well, the American dollar is rapidly becoming the Black Peter (or in North American terms, the 'Old Maid') of international currency."

"But the American dollar has the full wealth of America behind it," my banker friend said. "Why on earth do we have to support it with yellow metal? It costs us a lot of money to guard it in our vault."

"Actually," I said, "the reverse is true. It is the yellow metal that is the real wealth and guards your money outside the vault."

Over ten years have passed. Recently my banking friend phoned to say that he was retiring. "You know," he told me, "when I cleaned out my desk I found the deck of cards you left in my office. I'd like to keep them as a reminder that you were one of the first to realize that American bankers were playing Black Peter with the U.S. dollar."

Bankers, of course, are never popular. When they succeed and build tall glass mausoleums, depositors grumble, "This is our sweat." When they fail and indulge in crazy loans, the depositors scream, "You cheated us." Today, however, the depositors' enmity is largely justified. A bankrupt industry is trying to cover its true circumstances to justify further borrowing, and the main actors are the largest American bankers.

Anyone who reads the daily statements and comments of international bankers and familiarizes himself with words and expressions such as "dislocation," "rescheduling," "nonoperative loans" and "nonperforming loans" wonders what the world would do without dictionaries. For example, 95 percent of the interest that Poland "agreed" to pay for its defunct loans will be plowed back. . . . into Poland. In other words, in 1983 the banks got only 5 percent of the interest owed. "Rescheduling" is just another word in modern international banking jargon for bankruptcy. It sells well on balance sheets in an attempt to convince gullible depositors that the assets of their trusted banking institutions are solid.

Presidents of the largest New York banks try to calm the public by telling them, "A sovereign nation can never die," and therefore, "There is no such thing as a bad loan to a government." They cover up the fact that all of them, without exception, are being held up by Brazil, Mexico, Cuba, Poland, Argentina and Romania, to name just a few. Western banks are being told by sovereign nations, "You had better continue to support us; otherwise we shall sink together."

Recently the *Wall Street Journal* carried an article about Bankers Trust of South Carolina, a small Mom-and-Pop bank that was sharked in the network of loan syndication to Mexico. In 1981 the bank wanted to be fashionable and make big money on small loans to developing countries. It put $5 million in a short-term loan syndicated by the New York banks, which has been turned by Mexico into a never-paying affair.

Richard Fearrington, the senior vice-president of the bank, deserves a medal, not for falling into the Mexican net, but rather for being able to admit to the naïveté with which his bank marched into the trap. With uncharacteristic and engaging frankness he admits that neither he nor the other six members of his bank's credit committee could establish the credit-worthiness of Mexico prior to extending the loan. All they knew was that the big boys—Chase Manhattan, Citibank, Morgan Guaranty Trust and Chemical Bank —were lending money to Mexico. They reasoned if it was good for the giants of New York, it must be good for the little guys.

Bankers Trust of South Carolina would not have hit the *Wall Street Journal* had our Mr. Fearrington not started to push Mexican representatives in New York, advising them that he was not willing to roll over the short-term credit into a continuous financial sausage. When he became stubborn, Manufacturers Hanover Trust intervened and, according to Mr. Fearrington, "acquainted" him with the situation; he then realized that suing Mexico for $5 million would have been, in his own words, like "squeezing blood from a turnip."

The shocking part of the trials and tribulations of Bankers Trust of South Carolina (which is not related to Bankers Trust of New York) was that in our age of modern communications, it had to rely on newspapers and newscasts to learn about the noncredit-worthiness of Mexico. Small banks are kept in the dark by their big brothers and the only consolation to Bankers Trust is that now it is mentioned in the same breath as BankAmerica, Bank of

Tokyo, Banca Nazionale del Lavoro, Chase Manhattan, Citibank, Manufacturers Hanover Trust, the Royal Bank of Canada—the list goes on and on. They had to squander $5 million to be admitted to the big boys' club.

The sorry story of Bankers Trust is indicative of the fate of the banking industry as a whole. On the morning after the credit expansion orgy, 1,500 of the 15,000 American banks found themselves involved in sour loans. U.S. Treasury Secretary Donald Regan admits that those banks who lent money to Latin America are in virtually every state and every congressional district. The unbridled craze was a mixture of greed and ignorance. One wisely foolish small-town banker admits why he stayed out of Zaire. "Hell, I didn't even know where Zaire was." (His ignorance of geography is shared by some top White House aides. Remember Judge William Patrick Clark, the candidate who replaced Richard Allen as National Security Advisor? Clark admitted in his Congressional hearing that he was not sure where Zimbabwe was or who the prime minister of South Africa was, although the gentleman happened to be visiting the United States that very week.)

Politicians can always maintain that they leave to the bureaucrats such nit-picking as facts as the whereabouts of countries and the names of their prime ministers. For bankers, such ignorance can be very costly indeed.

The stupidity of greedy banks was best demonstrated a few years ago when a bank in California was conned into extending American dollars for a 10 million mark note issued in 1923. The bank was so keen to enter the field of foreign exchange, and so impressed with the bill dating back to the Weimar Republic and Germany's glorious days of hyperinflation, that it did not bother to find out that the big fancy bill bought only an inland postal stamp or a box of matches in 1923. Today such banknotes are solely good as wall decorations.

The problems with the banks have barely started to surface. The information and the scare stories now emerging about potential defaults are tantamount to those of a mass murderer whose first skeleton has been unearthed and who, after being convicted, admits to 20 additional killings. Then the grisly evidence is unraveled on a daily basis.

Nonperforming Loans

Business corporations, banks and government agencies are in the same situation. Financial analysts and critics of the banking industry have addressed themselves only to the obvious: that technically many major American banks are, at best, insolvent and, at worst, bankrupt. This is highlighted by the fact that the banks cannot afford to write off loans of defaulting debtors because removing an asset from the balance sheet will reveal the true picture. Therefore, the sour loans must be kept in a "nonperforming" category.

The lost loans carry enough hope of redemption to leave them on paper, yet they are just enough removed from causing an official declaration of bankruptcy, which would trigger a run on the banks. The "nonperforming" label holds back a domino effect looming over the entire industry.

Now, a regulation has been adapted that requires American banks to report quarterly on all loans 30 days or more past due. No wonder the banks vigorously opposed it. The banks brought the present administration to power. It was the best bureaucracy money could buy. However, American and Canadian banks have shifted the responsibility of reporting to overseas and offshore branches, which are immune from harsh reporting procedures.

The regulation overlooks an important element in establishing the creditability of any bank: its involvement in ever-accommodating letters of credit, which are never reported in balance sheets. A bank collects between 1 percent and 3 percent commission on letters of credit, which are created to make sure that the date of shipment and condition of goods will be according to the contract.

The short-term conventional commercial letter of credit does not pose a great problem to a bank. The bank will be called upon to pay only if the ordering or the receiving party has defaulted on preagreed commitments. Great difficulties with letters of credit arise when substantial international loans, particularly from shaky regimes and semigovernmental agencies, are coming due and need to be covered in haste.

For example, say that the Nigerian Tourist Development Corporation has failed to meet a $20 million loan to Citibank. Citibank has to report the loan as past due and consequently move the $20 million from its assets column to its liabilities column, which translates into a $40 million difference. Should the Nigerian Corporation, however, by agreement with Citibank, provide a letter of credit from, say, the First National Bank of Abeakuta, guaranteeing that the loan will be paid on the first of May, 1995, not only will the loan not move from the nonperforming past into the liabilities column, it will now become a fresh, good and shiny asset as before. It will be garnished with interest, and the banks will declare it as a profitable transaction. The international manager of Citibank will be able to report to his committee that he has a letter of credit from the Abeakuta Bank.

The fact that the Tourist Corporation is already the largest debtor of the Nigerian Bank, owes it already the equivalent of $40 million and is bankrupt four times over does not change the "fact" that Citibank now has a letter of credit from another bank, which will satisfy the books for the next decade. Black Peter has been passed on to another player, and the world at large is none the wiser.

If undermining the U.S. dollar was only a domestic problem, if only American banks were playing Black Peter, perhaps, just perhaps, something could be done. But the problem of the dollar as viewed by Europeans is that American currency by design and circumstance has become *the* reserve of every nation on earth. American paper, a liability of Uncle Sam, has become the asset of the rest of the world. In practical terms, the Federal Reserve Bank is the World Bank.

The dollar was good, even hoarded, as long as everyone accepted and believed that U.S. currency had a trusted and respected foundation. Today, however, Europeans consider the dollar less and less acceptable as a reserve currency, despite its recent strength. The Germans say the dollar is *kaputt*. The *Washington Post*, the *Wall Street Journal* and hundreds of newspapers and TV commentators tell the world that the liabilities of Uncle Sam by far exceed his assets. Once again, two and two make five.

Even if the domestic debt load of Uncle Sam were "only" $1.7 trillion—and by some calculations it is much larger—it would take over 1,500 years to repay the principal at the rate of $1 billion per year. Those who own a large enough computer can calculate the interest. To believe that over the next two to five years the U.S. dollar can survive in its present form and continue to play its present international role is, in the minds of European experts, an exercise in hopelessness.

In June 1982, the heads of the world's seven Western industrial powers met at Versailles. When it came to voting on crucial money matters, the participants voted with their thumbs. In September 1982, at the great IMF money jamboree in Toronto, participants voted with their fists. In recent months, diplomacy and good manners have eroded; voting is now conducted with feet. Only days after the splendor of Versailles, France's foreign minister, Claude Cheysson, summed it all up in Rome. He observed that, "A gradual divorce between the United States of America and Europe is taking place." The partnership that has lasted for nearly 40 years is coming to an end.

Was Mr. Cheysson's Rome statement a *ballon d'essai*—a trial balloon—to gauge the tempers in Washington, or was it a result of the *basta*—enough—that the Italians shouted as they pounded the table? One thing is clear: the *Annus Mirabilis*, the year of wonder, of new promised practical experiments in economics, is no longer acceptable to Europeans. The fact that European politicians are also governing by public opinion polls only underlines the problem. Europe's political practicality is the same as it is across the ocean. Politicians everywhere make political capital out of the warning, "*Après nous, la déluge.*" The politicians may not know much about building arks, but they do know the flood is on its way. The public at large is afraid to associate itself with a loser. In its eyes the dollar and the United States are inseparable.

The whispering in Versailles grew into a bickering in Toronto and other international conferences. To save their political hides at home, delegates demanded a reduction in U.S. interest rates. Federal Reserve Board Chairman Paul Adolph Volcker succumbed to the pressure and a so-called "stronger" dollar surfaced on foreign exchanges. Interest rates dropped and euphoria swept the financial markets of North America.

A "strong" dollar turned out to be good for public relations but bad for U.S. exports. Whatever tinkering and "fine-tuning" politicians in the United States did with the printing press, the U.S. dollar was eleventh in terms of industrial competitiveness. Data compiled by Citibank confirmed that the sole export that the United States can conduct now without competition is selling on credit to the Russians and the Third World countries, pouring export products and grain into a bottomless sack of already bankrupt customers.

The recent history of American grain sales to Russia shows the bankruptcy of American economic policy. President Jimmy Carter got mad at the Russians when they moved into Afghanistan. He stopped their American grain supply, hoping that a combative hard line would keep him in power. Carter was not reelected, and the Russians are still in Afghanistan.

The grain embargo was past history soon after the Reagan administration took office.

During late October 1982, when it became apparent that the United States had a bumper grain crop, an official of the Department of Agriculture was "hoping" that the Russians would buy American grain. "Staying the course" soon turned into an embarrassingly quick resumption of grain supplies to the U.S.S.R. Moreover, in spite of great financial difficulties within the Eastern bloc and a good chance that moneys owed will never be repaid, grain is now sold *on credit* to the Soviet Union. Credit sales mean that political talk about needy Russians depleting already empty Russian foreign reserve coffers is hogwash. The U.S. policy has left its allies confused and has gained nothing.

American policy regarding Russia's natural gas pipeline from Siberia also has left Europeans bewildered, even after American sanctions were lifted and the economic saber-rattling ended. In spite of initial American opposition and talk that slave labor is being used in its construction, its installation was not interrupted for even one day; the pipeline, the largest trade deal in history, is creeping into Europe. Italians, West Germans, the French, Austrians and even the Swiss are now using Russian gas. Within six years the Russians will be supplying 35 percent of Italy's gas consumption, 34 percent of West Germany's and 26 percent of France's, all at above-market prices. Poland and Czechoslovakia will also be enjoying the pipeline, financed by Europe directly and the United States indirectly.

Here is the practical situation. The gas reserves are and will remain Russian. The pipe now on Russian soil is effectively Russian. The pipe outside Russian soil will receive its gas from Russia. The pipeline's Western European and American financiers hope to be repaid at 8 percent interest. The payments, if any, will be in kind. West German banks will no doubt tout the "benefits" of the pipeline to the public and exert pressure on their government to keep the gas taps open as long as possible—all to ensure that the Russians will be able to repay the crumbling German banks. Western Europe will have to pay above-market prices for gas so the Russians can repay loans at below-market interest rates.

The Reagan administration's opposition to the pipeline sank without a trace. Europeans were convinced once more that U.S. policy is a weak reed upon which to lean. The European public has begun to realize that it can expect very little help from Uncle Sam, who needs all his charity at home. The reality of being unprotected has brought about a greater tolerance, almost affection, for the Russian bear by Western Europe. The Spanish and the Portuguese are only the most recent to cast their ballots for "Better Red than dead."

In their relationships with their more powerful neighbors, Europeans have that agility of bitten dogs, which comes with many centuries of experience: they know when to run. When they sense that their opponent is about to off-load Black Peter onto them again, they leave the table.

Because the emaciation of the U.S. dollar has weakened currencies throughout the world, there is no longer just one Black Peter in the global card game. When the entire deck is made up of Black Peters, the only winners will be the ones who manage to unload their cards for something of real value and get out of the game. The losers will then be stuck with piles of worthless paper adorned with pictures no more valuable than the face of the smiling chimney sweep.

Protectionism

Russia, in the eyes of Europe, has emerged as the winner in all recent confrontations with the United States. The Siberian gas pipeline was just one of many victories. America's grain embargo was lifted by the White House on the day that Yuri Andropov, Russia's ex-police boss, was named head of the Communist party, the top Soviet post. A dozen countries that were united flimsily through fear of Russia are now, in the tradition of European survivalism, looking for a protector.

Vocal Europeans have convinced the United States that conducting trade with Russia, and even absorbing bad debts from time to time, is cheaper than going to war. Passing some honey to the hungry Russian bear may keep him away for a while. It is also a form of added cost of living. Protectionism has always been a way of life in both the Western and Eastern sectors of Europe. Europeans want hope *now*, and they have been sold on the idea that compromise with Russia is the one out of two options they dislike the least.

By his own admission, Uncle Sam is no longer the world's policeman; Vietnam finished that. America's remaining global influence was, at the end of the Vietnam War, attributed to the dollar. The new reality is that the dollar is also being defeated by serious problems besetting the U.S. economy.

Europeans now fear the United States will attempt to cure the economic havoc accelerated during recent years through exchange controls and social programs. They cite Great Britain, with unemployment at 13 percent, as an example of restrictions. They fear U.S. leaders will be pinned down attempting to cope with an army of unemployed over 8 million strong, as her basic industries decline and her economy slips toward yet another recession. Another army of 25 million unemployed has now amassed in the rest of the Western world.

A recent meeting of the General Agreement on Tariffs and Trade (GATT) in Geneva highlighted the utter distrust among partners. Long-standing trade agreements are coming apart and are about to be buried under a wall of new protectionism. No trading partner can any longer tolerate or accommodate the constant cheating they all engage in: each feels that it has not cheated enough to get its fair share of the pie.

European financiers overwhelmingly believe that the Republican Party can retain political power only by employing the same remedy prescribed by the Democrats: the printing press. History books are full of empires that shrunk into provinces because of currency debasements.

Eurodollar bankers, whose main focus, contrary to the misleading name, is North America, know better; but they cannot afford to turn off the spigot. It is common knowledge that a $100 billion annual surplus of the Organization of Petroleum Exporting Countries (OPEC) ran into a deficit in 1982, 1983, 1984 and 1985. The bankers cannot blow the whistle on their own business.

Their debtors are at best prepared to replace paper that they owe with more paper that they intend to owe.

The public has been duped into believing that rescheduling of loans brings everything under control, that a miracle cure has been found and that a stroke of a pen or punch on a computer key can turn nothing into something. But the huge failures of international corporations already are being whispered in executive suites in Zurich, London and New York. The possible domino effect of bankruptcies has only been removed temporarily from the front page of the daily paper.

All recorded lending binges have resulted in armed conflict. When too many people become debtors, they are on the lookout for a superficial excuse to justify living on borrowed funds. Parasitism becomes respectable when debtors believe that the money extended to them is actually owing to them.

We have first-hand confirmation of this here on our own doorstep. Mexico's President José Lopez Portillo, who led his country into its present economic disaster, found the reason for the turmoil on the eve of his departure from office: the bankers must have drained the economy. So he nationalized their banks; during one weekend he confiscated $12 billion of hard currency deposits in Mexican banks. From the lectern of the United Nations' General Assembly, he preached to his creditors: "Payment's suspension is to no one's advantage and no one wants it .... Today Mexico and many other countries of the Third World are unable to comply with the period of payments agreed upon. ... We cannot paralyze our economies or plunge our people into greater misery in order to pay a debt on which servicing tripled without our participation and with terms that are imposed on us .... We countries of the South are about to run out of playing chips and we cannot stay in the game. This will end in defeat for everyone."

In plain language President Lopez Portillo, who retired into a new multimillion-dollar mansion overlooking Mexico City, was hinting to the world and to some 300 American banks that financed his country that Mexico does not intend to pay its debts. So much for the myth that sovereign nations "always pay." How about some colorful Mexican bonds to decorate your walls? They will blend well with some other wallpaper depicting Chiang Kai-shek, the Kaiser or a bearded Romanoff.

International bankers recently downgraded the credit rating of 105 countries that were assessed during 1980, 1982 and 1984. Potential borrowers lost on an average 8 points of merit; the quality of the average global borrower is now 45 points out of 100. Some countries under review lost 20 to 30 points in the span of two years. Would you do business with an entity that offers you at best a 45 percent chance of recovering your investment?

The threat of default is so massive that the large banks, already up to their eyebrows in debts owing by developing countries, continually extend further loans to their already bankrupt clients. These loans represent twice the capital reserves of the banks involved. A few years ago a nation in a financial bind would come hat in hand to the IMF or whisper discreetly to world bankers for help. The neighbors in the rest of the world were not supposed to know. Today, the international debt plungers cover 80 percent of the world map. How long will creative accounting and "rescheduling," "unproductive loans" and other newly created falsifications be able to shore up the economic tumult?

The vulnerability of the international banking system tends to be overlooked by many of us. A small bank in Oklahoma or Tennessee that goes broke, of course, makes headlines and TV specials; financial correspondents keep on munching at it for weeks. Spicy details about the large, privately-owned Italian bank Banco Ambrosiano, whose chairman was found hanging under a bridge across the Thames, titillated the public for weeks.

When you deal with a bank which has its roots in your community and it goes bankrupt, you as an individual stand to lose what you accumulated in the past, except for what the FDIC is able to pay in bailout money. When you deal with an international institution, you forfeit what you may make in the future as a nation on top of your own loss.

Banks are more vulnerable than most people realize. After all, they "own" only the moneys that have been deposited by their clients. Depositors receive interest payments only as long as the wisdom and rationale of bank management is sound and borrowers repay their loans, plus interest. Depositors lose if the manager is ignorant, goes berserk or is an embezzler.

In recent decades Switzerland has become synonymous with international banking. A horde of bankers of every nationality has maintained that what is good for the Swiss is good for everyone. Data based on figures from the Bank of International Settlements in Basel reveal that international credits granted by the banks reached $1,542 trillion at the end of 1981, an increase of 40 percent within two years. That's $1,542,000,000,000. This is $4,000 for every man, woman and child on earth. Since 60 percent of the inhabitants of this planet account for less than $70 U.S. per capita per annum, the burden of the $1,542 trillion rests with the still-affluent West.

The international debt has been hatched by international banks of American, Canadian, German and French bankers, who turned the $1,542 trillion international debt into a concoction of misery in which everyone is involved. The Polish debt of $27 billion is mere petty cash.

Switzerland participates in this incredible market to the extent of $162 billion U.S., 10.5 percent as a lender and 2.2 percent as a borrower, with a net creditor position (namely, moneys owing to our favorite Swiss banks) of $128 billion or $200,000 per capita. Americans and Canadians are much worse off: on top of huge subsidies to foreign nations for military and altruistic reasons, they also have the squandering and budget imbalances of their own politicians.

The chairman of Union Bank of Switzerland made no bones about the crisis presently looming over the international banking system: "International banking has in general deteriorated ...

vulnerability has increased considerably as a result of greater instability on the international, political and economic scenes. Risk assessment has become more difficult, because a quick and often unexpected change of character and potential of risks is constantly taking place."

Pessimists and optimists differ in opinion only with regard to the time that a tremor in the international banking system will take to throw the entire global banking system into disarray. Even the smallest Savings and Loan or Caisses Populaires will not be spared. Pessimists maintain that it may be a matter of seconds; optimists hope there will be an advance warning of several hours. But all agree that a shake-up in global banking is about to occur.

A crucial but logical conclusion is that only real money, namely the type which cannot arbitrarily be printed, legalized or outlawed, will buy goods and services. Moreover, in a banking calamity even holdings in safety deposit boxes in certain countries may be affected; therefore, only real money, such as precious metals tucked away in private depositories or hidden in a backyard, may escape the ravages of fallout.

Trying to make money on money will come to an abrupt halt. On that day, the seemingly expensive items held in a private depository may prove to be the wisest investment decision of a lifetime.

Eventually, today's players in the poker game of international finance will be called upon to show what is actually in their hand. Imagine the reaction when it becomes apparent that each one is the proud owner of a full house of five Black Peters. There is no honesty left, even among thieves.

Europeans believe that the game has been overplayed to such an extent that no soft talk or public relations campaign can cure it. Rescheduling proposals will be answered with an emphatic "No." A completely new game is in the offing, in which today's losers will have to ante up some real chips or leave the tables.

5
THE BANKS
AND THE CARTELS

*"In times of revolution, authority remains
with the greatest scoundrels."*
—GEORGES-JACQUES DANTON

Cartels become a reality when individuals, usually speaking the same language and wearing the same old school ties, coalesce to produce less of their common product at the expense of a gullible public. They dispense with costly promotions, avoid price wars and set and enforce the highest price the market can bear for their product. Once involved in a cartel, the happy band enjoys the well-being and protection of one single-price blanket. They all remain comfortable until one or more of the partners takes more than his share of the blanket for himself, leaving the others out in the cold.

Members of a cartel also become disarrayed and no longer speak with one voice when the objectives of the cartel splinter. It depends whether the easy money is channeled into casinos or used to feed tens of millions of impoverished inhabitants. Some of the oil-producing nations have partly invested the money extracted from the West over the past decade in grandiose five- and seven-year projects. They have become hooked on more and more dollars which, contrary to their pipe dreams, have become scarcer over the years. They now have to sell three times more oil than three years ago to a market that, at least temporarily, has turned into a free market based on supply and demand.

Bickering over production cuts in 1983 further brought harsh reality to the cartel. OPEC has never really worked. A decade ago, as well as now, OPEC countries were completely dependent on the shipping facilities of the consuming nations. In their rush to make petrodollars work, none of the Persian Gulf nations acquired even one tanker. Instead, they indulged in and enjoyed the merry-go-round of the recycling miracle of their petrodollars. As a result, oil producers are not only dependent on the consuming countries when it comes to shipping their oil across oceans, they also depend on the international banking system for recycling their dollars.

Observing the circus surrounding OPEC meetings leaves one with the unequivocal feeling that decisions with regard to oil production cuts and quotas are made neither in Riyadh, Tripoli nor Lagos. The decisions are made by huge banking interests, and the final decision reached need not be the most convenient one for the oil producers or for the consuming public of the West. The decision will be the one which suits the bankditos who started the money miracle.

During the past decade, the ever-escalating prices of crude oil have created the biggest banking boom in history. Big oil companies, encouraged by international banking interests, have created Middle East conflicts and wars, the most significant being the Yom Kippur War in 1973, which sent oil prices soaring. Now, 12 years later, the pawns in the game realize that their function was limited to producing money for the oil companies and the bankers.

Here are some of the highlights of this process. First, renewed conflict between Israel and the Arabs was created. The Arabs then declared an oil supply shortage, which allowed prices to rise from $3 per barrel to over $34 per barrel in little more than seven years. The West, dependent on Arab oil, had to pay the higher prices. The Arabs earned billions of dollars in oil emoluments, which gave birth to the petrodollar.

Billions of dollars extorted from "Little Me's" in consuming countries had to be rechanneled to keep the financial system working. Part of that money went to the oil-producing countries, but most had to be managed. Poor developing countries, which were the first victims of the universal oil price hike, received loans to subsidize the new oil prices and indulge in various development plans. The happy process flowed through the international banking mill, and the banks were made flush with tremendous profits, ping-ponging petrodollars to and fro. The producing countries were happy, because they earned more and more and, for several years, turned oil into a weapon and into a monetary instrument at the same time.

Later, the bankditos, along with the big oil companies, assumed correctly that when the oil embargo was announced, no one from the consuming nations would have the guts to tell the producing countries to drink their oil. The banks and big oil companies had adequate political clout to make the entire West succumb to blackmail. Their public relations machinery even made some people start to believe that the whole process was not so bad after all.

While the great petrophobia remains alive, well and crisscrossing the globe between Riyadh, Caracas and Vienna, the world at large has almost come to like those smiling ministers of fuel. Public opinion is being forged to fear the dissolution of OPEC as a greater calamity than the benefits that may be derived from falling prices of crude oil. The message of doom has actually made a petrofied world start to believe that the gang of 13 OPEC extortionists has all of a sudden become responsive to the concerns of the rest of the world. Accordingly, runs the propaganda, we should all run to our politicians and ask for or even demand higher prices for oil. We must make sure that OPEC does not fold. If OPEC goes, Mexico, Nigeria and Indonesia will be unable to pay their international debts. The banks will then fold, and a much greater calamity will occur. The failure of OPEC will cause a tidal wave of red ink, which will be followed by blood in the streets.

Who was, and still is, behind that hysterical campaign? The big banks, which have already been dispossessed of their wealth through foolishly extended "greed loans," and which have become famous for throwing good money after bad during the last decade, frantically pressure their political friends to yield to the perpetual blackmail of big oil, the most powerful lobby of our time. Niccolò Machiavelli's maxim, "It is more secure to be feared than to be loved" has become the order of the day.

The result of the 1982 IMF conference in Toronto underscored the ballooning of this powerful lobby. The outcome of the conference was predictable: it was decided that the poor in the rich countries would be taxed more in order to satisfy the pleasure of the rich in the poor countries.

The already nervous financial markets tend to get the jitters whenever new rumors circulate that short-term oil moneys deposited with U.S. and Western banks are about to be recalled. The circular logic attached to such a scenario is that in the absence of a smooth rollover, a general Western banking apocalypse is imminent. With oil prices falling, the danger that these funds will be withdrawn to pay current expenses grows every day. The debtors' blackmail usually works. Diplomats who sometimes have difficulty explaining the location of their newly created countries know only too well that Western banks—in effect you and I, the depositors—have become prisoners of their own credit.

These scenarios, involving a potential stoppage of the rollover game, have been conjured up by alarmist bankers and have taken over good reason and logic. In 1985, as well as ten years earlier, the main ingredients of reality seem to be overlooked. A decade ago no one dared to tell OPEC to drink their threats and subject themselves to a free market. Now somehow no one dares to tell them that if they withdraw their funds en masse from certain banks and cause an accelerating cash outflow, they will be the final holders of the empty bag. Amidst the crisis at hand also lurks opportunity. The American bankers have not asked themselves, "Where will the money be rolled over if it is taken out of New York?"

The OPEC countries may find that the assets and net worth of Swiss and German banks are made up of certificates of deposits of

American banks, which in turn have Polish, Romanian, Brazilian and Mexican paper. The Arabs will conclude that a domino effect will occur if they try to yank the rug out from under the American banks. The incumbent petrobarons may find out that if they really squeeze, they will have to try to collect their oil money directly from Poland and Brazil. OPEC may be greedy, but it is not so stupid as to risk the possibility of facing a court in session under a palm tree in Africa or even traveling to Warsaw, Prague or Budapest to have its day in court.

A set of circumstances created through the reality of free-market forces triggered by the deregulation of oil prices in the United States, which the present administration may take some credit for, has brought about the disarray in the ranks of OPEC. Before long, it will be realized that oil has ceased to be a weapon that can be used indefinitely. The reality that it has to be pumped out of the ground and carted to the pumps of the West and sold to Western consumers at now competitive prices is a dimension that has been overlooked for the past ten years. Encouraged and stimulated by the big oil companies and banks, the ever-growing greed of the producers has brought about their own downfall. OPEC has dug its own grave.

By the year 2000, as fantastic as it may seem now, the cruel sand and dust may rule over the vast deserts of Arabia once more. The great wealth of the past will have proved to be just another *fata morgana* for the storytellers in the black tents of the Bedouin. The camel, the ship of the desert, will once more be returned to its full glory. An Arab financier told me recently, "We well deserve it. We have contravened Koran dictates not to earn interest on money by giving out our oil emoluments to Western banks. We have sinned and are justly being punished."

While the original OPEC members are engaged in a cacophony of price cutting, a new, much stronger OPEC is forging ahead and crystallizing. It has taken little time for the newly assembled debtor class to discover its immense power. The members of this group speak the same language—need—and they wear the same outfit—bare feet and rags. It is they who are now dictating the terms of loan repayments, rather than those who give them the money. Cash is no longer king; the debtor is king.

The cartel of debtor nations rules through the one word that the entire Western banking community fears most: "default." The default of Mexico, Brazil and others will set up an avalanche, the size of which is difficult to imagine. No one financial institution in the world, no one currency, will remain unaffected. The great crisis will start on Wall Street, not in Brasília or Buenos Aires.

The problem is the U.S. dollar. The price of oil is denominated in dollars, and to the delight of certain financial planners, the dollar has become the only reserve currency of the world. If one day we find that the Russians were actually behind this plot, we should not be surprised. Having the dollar as the reserve currency of the world shifted the burden now facing the banks to those who create dollars in the United States, namely the Federal Reserve. The Federal Reserve cannot create money unless it issues certain financial instruments, which the public eventually pays for. The bottom line is that the American taxpayer is now facing the harsh reality that he has to pay for failing projects in Tanzania, bridges which lead nowhere in Brazil, aid programs for Bangladesh and maybe even for Russian armaments channeled to Cuba and now pointed at the United States and Central America. Nicaraguan troops and El Salvadorian rebels are using American weapons left over from the Vietnam War, which were captured by the victorious Communist forces.

For the banks, the greatest problem at the moment is to avert a run. When the public learns that America's nine largest banks are probably insolvent, and possibly bankrupt, a run on the banks will no doubt begin. This would have a worldwide effect. If you consider the deceit with which bankers now are trying to cover their foolish, greedy actions of the past few years, it is quite clear that they are preparing for the worst.

A BankAmerica spokesman said recently that his bank's exposure in Mexico represents only 2.3 percent of its outstanding debt.

What he forgot to mention is that the 2.3 percent figure applies to the total Mexican debt. This represents the lion's share of the entire assets of the BankAmerica in two countries, Brazil and Mexico, to whom the bank has extended loans totaling $4.8 billion. The value of the BankAmerica's total assets is only $4.2 billion. Thus, the bank is in the hole to these two debtors alone by approximately $600 million, give or take a few hundred million. The Brazilians and Mexicans have become the spokesmen of a hopelessly indebted Third World.

Carlos Langoni, the chairman of Brazil's central bank, has let it be known that some 125 United States banks hold 90 percent of Brazil's debt. In 1983, American banks gave a New Year's present of $1 billion to Brazil. To speed delivery of the bounty, President Reagan was asked to carry the check in person to Brasília aboard Air Force One. The bribe was ceremonially accepted, and peace in the banking community was restored for two weeks. The American delegation had hardly returned, however, when Brazilian envoys arrived in New York demanding that American banks reschedule the $80 billion then owing to them or face a formal default. Brazil now owes around $100 billion.

Overlooking Rio de Janeiro is a magnificent statue of Jesus on the Cross. One of the Brazilian officials who carried the latest word to New York was asked when payment might be expected: "You have all seen Christ overlooking Rio de Janeiro. On the day that we shall pay, He has promised to clap His hands in appreciation."

Two billion dollars given in unseemly haste to Mexico was less well publicized than the gift to Brasília. This was after the Mexican government expropriated all foreign deposits over a weekend and cleaned out some 50,000 nonresidents who happened to have deposits in Mexican banks. Given the choice between helping the citizens whose savings had been confiscated or the big banks, the Reagan administration chose the banks.

The Mexicans for all intents and purposes are now running the American banks and tell them exactly when and if they will accept additional loans in order not to say, "We default." A default would mean that the loans given to Mexico, which appear as assets on the balance sheets of American banks, would be turned into liabilities. The banks themselves would go from profitable institutions to bankrupt businesses.

Out of all this emerges the inevitable conclusion that soon the financial world will be fed up with subsidizing its own execution, and living with the sole option of whether to use A.C. or D.C. for the electric chair. The mountainous debt incurred by the have-nots, through the mismanagement and greed of those who head the Western banks, is about to be absorbed by the Western governments. They will have no option but to nationalize the debt. We saw this with the interest payable by Poland. We may expect similar developments with the rest of the Eastern bloc, followed by South America and much of Africa.

Soon, the blackmailers, those who demand to be paid over and above what they owe in order not to declare bankruptcy, will be told "You *are* bankrupt." Only when the Polands and Brazils are placed in default will the beleaguered Western banking system be able to make a fresh start.

By nationalizing the terrible debts, the Western governments can hope to turn credits into a strategic material that, if wisely used, can have far more leverage than any other weapon. The present situation must change out of necessity. We must hope that Western governments, which helped bring the old cartel of the OPEC petrobarons under control, can eventually reign in the new cartel of debtors.

6
THE BANKS
AND PETRODOLLARS

"As a general rule, nobody has money who ought to have it."
—BENJAMIN DISRAELI

The United States has 5 percent of the population of the world but consumes nearly 30 percent of the world's energy production. The American oil industry consists of some 16,000 companies, including 18 major ones and some 12,000 independent producers. It employs about 1.7 million workers. The largest oil company is Exxon Corporation, with assets of $41.5 billion.

In the United States and in other Western countries, the oil lobby is possibly the best and most organized. No Western government can pass any legislation, be it a windfall profits tax or any other taxation or regulatory plan, without the prior consent of the industry itself. Contributions from officers and employees of oil companies, and indeed from the companies themselves, have helped elect politicians. However, they can be unseated from their comfortable salaries and cushioned chairs just as easily. They may scream in public and give their consent grudgingly, but the oil companies in the United States can live with the windfall profits tax. The oil and energy industry has become so strong in the West that the function of everyday life, not to mention the survival of politicians, often depends on it. The controversy surrounding the British TV production "Death of a Princess" in 1980 and the involvement of Mobil Oil in the campaign

71

against its showing are indicative of the power and influence of the oil empires.

The Iranian capture of the American embassy in 1979, which had no precedent in modern history, only underlines the leverage that the oil industry has on world politics and our enormous dependence on the energy coming from the Middle East. What the politicians failed to see was that the Iranian problem was not an isolated one. It was a problem that started in the early 1930s, when the Arabs discovered the vast value of their oil. It took them several decades to find the important role that they could play in world politics. The Western world, through its greed for profits, built the Middle East's production, refining and shipping infrastructure, but Eastern wisdom triumphed over Western greed. The Arabs let us do the job of building and developing an ever-growing dependence on imported oil and then in 1973 nationalized the corporations and quadrupled the price, all in less than ten days. Now, with an oil glut upon us, the problem appears to be keeping the price of oil propped up to avoid major shocks to the international banking system.

Diversification Until Time Runs Out

Falling oil prices mean that the oil companies, more than others, are concerned about the future. All the major oil corporations have diversified into other fields to a large degree in order to employ the enormous revenues that they earn in oil, and to guard against the new reality of lower world oil prices. Exxon has moved into coal, minerals (uranium, copper and lead), solar energy, electric motors, information systems and real estate. Mobil has expanded into coal, retailing, packaging, solar energy, real estate and printing. Texaco's diversifications are coal, uranium and real estate. These oil giants especially like to own newspapers and publishing companies, which serve two purposes. The first is to make money. Second, and more important, is to create a positive public relations image of the oil industry and to justify its maximizing of profits as long as possible.

Saudi Arabia, the world's largest petroleum exporter, has sought to increase its influence through the financially beleaguered International Monetary Fund. After pushing Third World nations to near-bankruptcy, the Saudis were approached for handouts and loans to be given to their victims and channeled through the IMF. The main benefit to the Saudis is that they have the *de facto* underwriting of the United States for loans given to developing countries. They will end up having the gratitude of the half-starved nations, while the IMF and the United States are faced with the unpopular and almost impossible task of trying to collect these loans from bankrupt economies. A further advantage for the Saudis and other OPEC suppliers is their increasing voting strength in the IMF. In 1981, it went from 1.7 percent to 3.5 percent, a jump from thirteenth to sixth place among IMF members. At the beginning of 1981, in terms of importance Saudi Arabia ranked immediately behind the United States, Britain, West Germany, France and Japan, surpassing Canada and Italy.

Nevertheless, OPEC rulers have an immediate problem. They know that a revolution simmers under the barrels of oil. The oil caliphs get richer, but most of the 100 million Muhammadans of the Middle East are eagerly waiting to share in the wealth. For the caliphs it is far more comforting to have their wealth pumped from their fields and tucked away in Europe. In their hearts, the Arabs know that the picnic must come to an end one day, just as oil prices eventually had to decline. In the meantime, they are trying to make their wealth as secure as possible by acquiring gold. This is why it is so difficult for them to cut production in times of surplus. Their 1985 quota of 17.5 million barrels per day (mbd) was some 3.5 mbd more than their current demands.

The first target of oil money was the real estate market, heavily oversold in France, Britain and the United States. However, only a small portion of petrodollars went there, because of the fear of nationalization or confiscation. A title deed is only a piece of paper when its owner may be declared *persona non grata*. Property may be expropriated in the same fashion as the Arabs dealt with the oil companies in their own countries. Also, the Arabs are well aware of the law of supply and demand. They do not like to make it obvious that too many dollars are buying too few hotels, farms or other investments.

Some petrodollars are invested in everyday goods: perfumes, TV sets, Rolls-Royces, etc. Such articles may give their owners prestige and make some dealers happy, but they represent only a small amount of the dollars now in Arab hands, even at today's lower prices.

In addition, the Arab rulers are prepared to bestow only so much of their wealth on the inhabitants of their kingdoms. They also will strictly limit the money used to purchase influence in developing countries. These leaders realize that they can increase the standard of living of their people only to a certain level, and they know that loans extended to the Third World are, in fact, grants that will never be repaid.

The Koran forbids Muslims to charge interest. Loaning moneys at discount rates is as frowned upon as quaffing whiskey. But nothing keeps a Muslim from capital gains, and an Arab friend of mine predicts a massive entry of petrodollars into commodities. "After all, where else can you gain leverage from ten cents on the dollar, which the commodity market offers?" he asked. Trading commodities, however, is a risky business; owning gold and other precious metals is not. We are now witnessing a barter of energy for gold.

Black Gold for Yellow Gold

In early 1980, the IMF revealed figures showing the per capita gold reserves, in millions of ounces, held by the industrialized Western oil-buying nations vis-à-vis the per capita holdings of the oil producers. Considering that a few years ago most of the land of the producing nations was either brush or sand dunes, and that most of their citizens lived below the poverty line, the growing figures of their gold holdings should be watched carefully.

One should not discount the possibility that the Russians will

74

strike direct deals with the Arabs to effect direct sales of gold to the oil-producing countries at negotiated prices. A secret transaction of 300 tons of gold was conducted between the Soviet Union and Saudi Arabia between the middle of July and the middle of September of 1979. By doing so, the Soviets have been able to find a source of cheap dollars for the purchase of grain and other necessities from the Western world without unduly suppressing the levels of the world gold market. Other similar "off the books" transactions have taken place between these countries and others who are not anxious to have their commercial dealings a matter of record.

For the Arabs, gold is not just the money of last resort. Gold, precious stones and other metals are the obvious answer to preserve their purchasing power. Gold is the best of two worlds: it is *halal*—sanctioned by Koranic laws—and at the same time builds a hedge against a possible depreciation of the U.S. dollar.

If we consider that, at $500 per ounce, the gold stock of the United States is worth well over $100 billion, with more than seven times that many worthless dollars in the world markets outside the United States, it will take only a little psychological triggering to cause complete chaos in currency markets. It may happen in the near future unless a massive revaluation of the U.S. dollar versus gold takes place and, at the same time, the U.S. economy presents a new, convincing posture of strength. The Arabs are ahead of us in realizing that paper IOUs will lose all their value. On that day when we will not need their oil, we will also be out of our gold.

Individuals can win only by doing what the Arabs are doing. Take the advice of Dr. Franz Pick, who said, "Sit on your gold and make a fortune with your fanny."

THE BASES
OF WEALTH

7
THE PYRAMID
OF REAL WEALTH

"When it is a question of money, everybody is of the same religion."
—VOLTAIRE

Much of this book deals with a discussion of wealth in terms of its symbols. It deals with money in the bank and what I think is wrong with the banking system. I talk about precious metals, trading commodities, the rise and fall of gold and silver prices, and of stock and bond prices, about "hard" assets and other items that help the shrewd investor preserve and even increase his wealth in terms commonly used to measure that wealth, dollars or ounces of gold.

But dollars, or even gold and silver, are not real wealth, although you need them to obtain real wealth. Real wealth is something tangible. It is either something we need or want to make our lives more pleasant, or even possible, or something that is readily exchangeable for things we need or want.

John Pugsley in *The Alpha Strategy* defines real wealth as: "All the real products produced by man from the raw materials of nature, and by the use of which he derives survival, comfort and pleasure." This tangible wealth can be anything. It is a car, a watch, a pair of shoes, food of any kind, a house, a book. But since we live in a complex society where even the most independent person can produce only a small fraction of what he needs, our definition of wealth must be expanded to include a store of value or a medium of exchange; in other words, money.

Paper money—currency—cannot occupy a permanent place on a pyramid of real wealth. So much paper money has come and gone over the years that its place on our pyramid can only be temporary. However, since virtually everything we own or consume is purchased with currency, we cannot ignore it either. Today, the U.S. dollar, Swiss franc, West German mark and the Japanese yen are considered "hard" currencies, and a more stable store of value than the Greek drachma, Indian rupee, Mexican peso or Portuguese escudo. But the definition of a hard currency changes. Thirty years ago the British pound and the French franc were considered hard currencies, and the German and Japanese currencies were not. But the British and French economies have weakened, and the German and Japanese economies have strengthened—and their currencies have weakened and strengthened with them.

Real wealth can be land and that which man puts on the land or takes from it. It can be a copper mine, a productive farm, an office building or a home. A business, such as a factory or a retail store, can produce real wealth, or the money with which to buy real things.

Stocks and Bonds

Stock certificates have often been thought of as real wealth. As this is being written, the U.S. and many other Western stock markets are at or near their all-time highs in dollar terms or in terms of the currency where the shares are traded. I recommend trading in stocks, particularly the Standard and Poor 500 averages, and in selected issues that I believe to be undervalued or overvalued at any given point. But buying stocks with the intention of holding them indefinitely is another matter altogether.

Another problem with stocks is that most investors have little if any idea exactly what the companies they "own" through their share certificates actually do. A cardinal rule in investing in stocks is that you must understand the stock. I never invest in stock where I have no access to the company's real balance sheet and data, or where I cannot participate in the direction of the company in some way. When it comes to gambling and diversification of investments, I consider energy stocks and stocks related to gold, uranium and platinum the best bets in short terms. But this is because I know something about these areas.

When you purchase a stock, you bet on the ability of the company's management to produce profits, which will enable that management to pay dividends to induce you to stay with your stock or to purchase more of it. When you invest in a foreign country, your risk is doubled. You have to trust that particular management and, at the same time, the political stability of that country.

Bonds are rather like stocks. Today, inflation is low and interest rates are high by the standards of the last ten to twenty years, and real, after-tax and after-inflation returns are currently available. However, I doubt that this happy state of affairs will continue for long, and I prefer to treat bonds as I do stocks—as a vehicle for trading, not a long-term investment.

If you believe that the very issuance of a bond is a sign of weakness on the part of the issuer, you should think twice before loaning your hard-earned money, be it to a government or a multibillion-dollar corporation. After all, the corporation did not invite you to purchase shares in their profitable business. They happen to be in need of money, and they have asked you to loan them some for a fixed rate of dollar income over a period of time. Although a bond is a "strong paper," having priority over common stock in its claim on earnings and assets, it is, nevertheless, still paper.

Rarely has any government or corporation really liquidated a bond. Instead, when a bond reaches maturity, another, much bigger bond issue of the same corporation or government will appear on the market. This new bond is meant to repay your bond and the bonds of your fellow investors. In many instances, you will just replace your matured bond with another piece of paper and the illusion that you have earned money. Eventually you will be handed yet another piece of paper to decorate your wall, and another good story for your grandchildren. In the long run, in the words of Dr. Franz Pick, a bond is "a certificate of *guaranteed* confiscation by the government or big corporate powers of your money."

It is true that there is money to be made on the stock and bond markets. If you buy stocks when prices are low and sell later when prices are higher, you will indeed have made a profit, especially if your return has exceeded the rate of inflation. If you have been paid dividends in the meantime, so much the better. If you buy bonds when interest rates are high, and sell them when interest rates are lower, you have likewise profited, especially if capital appreciation plus accumulated dividends exceed the inflation rate. But if you buy either with a view to holding them for the long haul, you are throwing your money away.

Any country can pass legislation to impose higher withholding taxes, restrict remittance abroad or nationalize an industry. Bonds and stocks are only pieces of paper, a promise to deliver a fixed return or a share of profits and capital appreciation, and the signature on such a paper is only as good as the person who signs it. I would invest in a small corporation run by one man, or a family business with a good record of prudent and steady development, rather than rely on the hot tips that the croupiers of the various stock or investment firms are giving.

Real wealth can be affected by inflation or recession. Inflation destroys paper claims on wealth—bonds, annuities, savings accounts and other debt obligations. Anyone who lends money for interest is a very likely loser in times of serious inflation. Recession or deflation has less effect on the value of so-called "hard" assets such as precious metals, gems and collectibles. Although these assets do not earn interest or produce real products, they serve as stores of value when financial instruments like stocks and bonds are suspect because of inflation, recession or an oppressive government that views the wealth of its citizens as the wealth of the state.

Food as Real Wealth

Today, stockpiling food is increasingly important for both physical and financial survival. Natural disasters such as floods, drought, tornadoes and even volcanic eruptions can cause food shortages almost overnight. Power failures can cripple our cities, interrupting electricity and transportation, and affecting food supplies. We can continue to expect business failures, high unemployment rates and strapped municipal governments. As a result of a defaulting monetary system, civic services are in danger of breaking down or being disrupted for long periods.

Miami and New York needed only a spark to burst into flames. An acquittal of a policeman accused of murdering a citizen in Miami and a blackout in New York caused havoc. Several million unemployed individuals can easily wind up on the streets in addition to the perennial hooligans. While the Establishment glibly announces yet another "New Prosperity," we learn that in Los Angeles and New York the total number of murders has escalated to over 2,000 per year.

There is no way of moving idle masses off the streets and into the production sphere except by war or hyperinflation. The advice of the prophets of gloom should be turned into profits of gloom: there is still time to buy your essential survival needs that shortly may be impossible to obtain or will cost very much more.

It is estimated that if food production stopped or transportation systems were interrupted, grocery stores would run out of fresh milk in a day or two. Eggs, red meat and poultry would be gone in a week. Then no amount of money could put food on your table. On the day the grocery store does not open, or the day after it has been looted, you need food, not just cash, Krugerrands or silver coins. Food is going to become a barterable commodity. The food will be real wealth, just like gold and silver.

Even if some food is still available in times of emergency, panic buying can be both costly and wasteful. Conventional foods, even if canned or stocked in a freezer, have a limited life. Besides, refrigeration is costly, consumes precious energy and relies on the public power supply. Fortunately for us, modern technology has come up with a solution to these problems: the process of freeze-drying food.

Today, a wide variety of excellent freeze-dried foods with long shelf lives is available. Three dozen cartons of freeze-dried food can last one person a full year. A family of four can store a year's supply of freeze-dried food in a large closet. The relatively new freeze-drying process has made plentiful, tasty and nutritious food available for long-term use.

In addition to freeze-dried foods, many foods can be purchased in bulk at a much lower price from your supermarket. Properly stored in a cool, dry and dark place, noodles and macaroni will last five years; rice and dried beans and peas will last ten years; honey, jams, jellies, sugar, syrup, salt and pepper, wheat, tea and hard liquor (gin, vodka, whiskey) will last indefinitely.

Many other products we use every day can be stored for future use to guard against inflation or something worse. These include hand tools (saws, knives, hammers, nails), all manner of paper products (napkins, towels, toilet tissue, writing paper, wrapping paper), flashlights, sports equipment (golf, baseball, tennis and football gear and equipment), plastic products, petroleum products (except gasoline) — the list is virtually endless. Basically, you can store anything that won't deteriorate over, say, five or ten years or longer.

You may want to acquire your own armory or electric generators, or buy an underground condominium. However, you may not want to be the only survivor on this planet or share it with some very dull neighbors who can afford to purchase into your cave boulevard. You should concentrate on surviving a temporary collapse or disruption of supply, and temporary breakdowns of community services. Having an adequate food supply is the best way to give yourself peace of mind. If you buy freeze-dried food today, you can fix the price of food and make your future a lot more secure at the same time.

And if you are suddenly faced with a stable world, then may

you, and all of us, be "disappointed" and eat the food that was stored away for a rainy day.

Pyramids of Wealth

I have prepared three pyramids of real wealth. One is a pyramid of what I believe is desirable to hold during inflationary times, another is for deflationary times and the third is for times of war and political instability.

One item is at the base of all three of my pyramids, and that is long shelf-life foods. Food storage is rarely discussed in terms of investment or wealth, mainly because in the West we have always taken plentiful and relatively inexpensive food for granted. But inflation, deflation and war have destroyed fortunes and people's lives overnight. Having an adequate supply of food on hand is the best way to insure your survival in times of economic or political instability.

My inflationary pyramid emphasizes tangible wealth and hard assets—items that should hold or even increase their purchasing power over time as currencies depreciate. While inflation is temporarily in check in North America and some of Europe, the residents of inflation-racked countries such as Argentina and Israel will always look beyond the "currencies" of their own country to find tangibles to preserve their wealth. They often preserve it in hard currencies, usually U.S. dollars. If a real, after-tax and after-inflation return is available, then liquid funds in hard currencies are very desirable during inflationary times.

Two other sound investments near the base of all three of my pyramids are money on deposit in a hard currency and precious metals securely held outside your country of residence. For most North Americans and Europeans, this means a U.S. dollar or Swiss franc bank account, and a safety deposit box at a Swiss bank. These can be invaluable in preserving your assets from your government and are a hedge against economic uncertainty at home, however sad a commentary this is on the state of economic and financial freedom available in the West.

I am also very bullish, long-term, on gold and silver. Their ultimate utility is as survival tools—as real money in times of hyperinflation or of war and political upheaval. They can also preserve your wealth in times of deflation. In a real depression, stocks and bonds can become worthless if the issuer goes bankrupt, but gold is always gold. It is one monetary asset that is not at the same time someone else's liability. If you hold gold, you are not dependent on a corporation to make a profit, a borrower to be able to make interest payments or a government to refrain from debasing its currency.

My inflationary pyramid has real assets at its base, and monetary assets such as stocks, bonds, annuities and insurance policies farthest away from the base. Here, real wealth is either something you can use—food, clothing, consumer goods and so on—or something you can use as money that will retain its value, such as precious metals.

Between precious metals and paper assets are those real assets that are less liquid or are less readily divisible than gold or silver, such as gems, artwork, other collectibles and real estate. Here the markets are thinner and liquidity is not guaranteed. The result is that the spread between what you will get if you sell and what you must pay when you buy is much greater.

Real estate or investment in a business is not as desirable as precious metals in inflationary times. We all need a job or a profession to generate current income and, one hopes, a surplus. But counting on a business or a real estate investment to retain its value and ability to earn income during inflation is risky. Wage and price controls, the bankruptcy of a major customer or supplier, rent controls and other external factors may cause an otherwise sound business or investment to become unviable.

A deflationary environment still calls for survival food, U.S. dollar or Swiss banking facilities and some gold in the form of bullion coins. But now selected financial instruments move much closer to the base of our investment pyramid. U.S. government obligations, when they pay a real, after-tax and after-inflation return, are as good as anything else in a period of deflation. Some of your wealth can even be kept in cash. These are spendable anywhere and offer complete privacy. Just above these investments are conservative and liquid money-market funds and top-quality corporate bonds that offer little risk of default.

Real estate and collectibles not readily convertible to cash become much less desirable in deflationary periods. Even owning your own home is a doubtful investment, as many houses that can't be sold are on the rental market, often at very desirable rates.

Times of war and political instability can play havoc with the financial and physical infrastructure of a country. Here, real estate, stocks and bonds, and other traditional investments can easily become worthless overnight. Consider Lebanon, where many manufacturing and other companies have simply ceased to exist due to the war and instability in that area. The former American embassy once provided its owner with a handsome rental income. Now, the unfortunate landlord is the proud owner of a pile of rubble.

Food, hard currency banknotes and precious metals must be at the base of your pyramid in unstable times. Also important, though not measurable as "wealth" in the same manner as other investments, is the ability to leave a danger zone. The inability to flee, either from lack of resources or lack of a destination, has cost many people their lives. Others more fortunate have merely lost their possessions.

The real estate most worth owning during war or political turmoil is your own home (assuming that it stays in one piece) or a working farm. Agricultural properties can be bartered for a ticket out of the country or seized outright. But farmland can also be a blessing: the luckiest Germans in 1945 and 1946 were the ones who owned and lived on their own farms. They were able to grow much of what they consumed and could barter for the rest.

Later chapters will deal in more detail with many of the specific items on these pyramids. Here, the three pyramids provide a readily accessible picture of the bases of real wealth.

THE PYRAMID OF REAL WEALTH:
I. THE INFLATIONARY SCENARIO

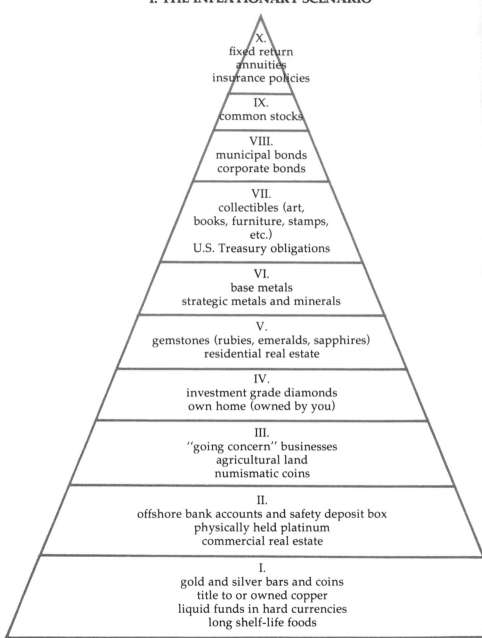

X.
fixed return
annuities
insurance policies

IX.
common stocks

VIII.
municipal bonds
corporate bonds

VII.
collectibles (art,
books, furniture, stamps,
etc.)
U.S. Treasury obligations

VI.
base metals
strategic metals and minerals

V.
gemstones (rubies, emeralds, sapphires)
residential real estate

IV.
investment grade diamonds
own home (owned by you)

III.
"going concern" businesses
agricultural land
numismatic coins

II.
offshore bank accounts and safety deposit box
physically held platinum
commercial real estate

I.
gold and silver bars and coins
title to or owned copper
liquid funds in hard currencies
long shelf-life foods

THE PYRAMID OF REAL WEALTH:
II. THE DEFLATIONARY SCENARIO

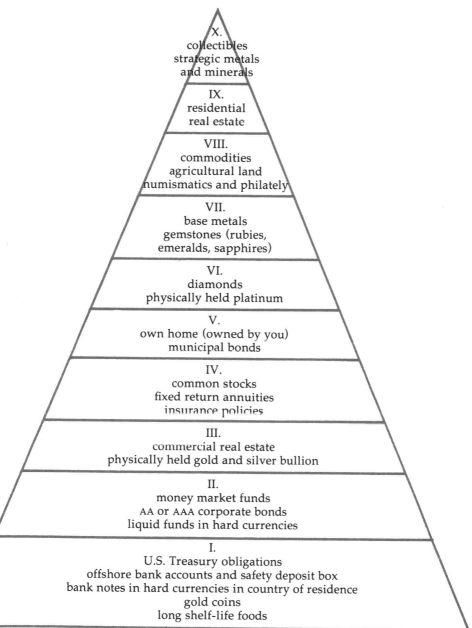

X.
collectibles
strategic metals
and minerals

IX.
residential
real estate

VIII.
commodities
agricultural land
numismatics and philately

VII.
base metals
gemstones (rubies,
emeralds, sapphires)

VI.
diamonds
physically held platinum

V.
own home (owned by you)
municipal bonds

IV.
common stocks
fixed return annuities
insurance policies

III.
commercial real estate
physically held gold and silver bullion

II.
money market funds
AA or AAA corporate bonds
liquid funds in hard currencies

I.
U.S. Treasury obligations
offshore bank accounts and safety deposit box
bank notes in hard currencies in country of residence
gold coins
long shelf-life foods

THE PYRAMID OF REAL WEALTH:
III. DURING TIMES OF WAR AND POLITICAL INSTABILITY

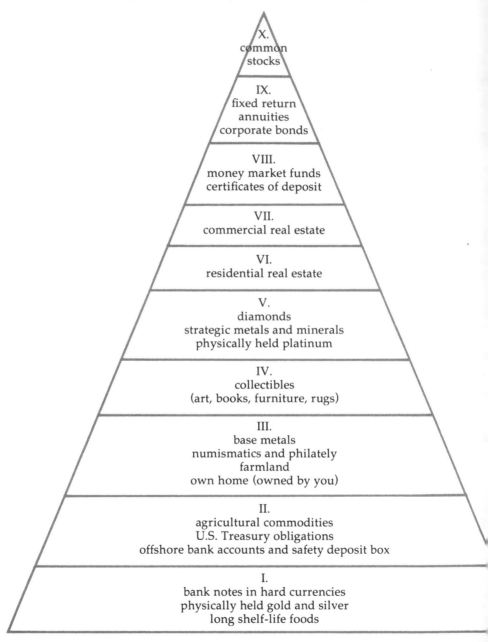

X.
common
stocks

IX.
fixed return
annuities
corporate bonds

VIII.
money market funds
certificates of deposit

VII.
commercial real estate

VI.
residential real estate

V.
diamonds
strategic metals and minerals
physically held platinum

IV.
collectibles
(art, books, furniture, rugs)

III.
base metals
numismatics and philately
farmland
own home (owned by you)

II.
agricultural commodities
U.S. Treasury obligations
offshore bank accounts and safety deposit box

I.
bank notes in hard currencies
physically held gold and silver
long shelf-life foods

8
GOLD AND MONEY

"Money costs too much."
—RALPH WALDO EMERSON

Money is only a means to an end. We have to make use of our money and purchasing power throughout our lifetime, enjoy it during our autumn days and leave some real money—not just paper—to our loved ones who survive us. In order to do so, we must first understand the nature of real money.

When human beings decided that they needed money, they visualized it performing certain major functions. It had to be a popularly accepted standard of value, an accepted method of payment, easily divisible, easily transportable and, most important, a store and source of value. By now, we all know that paper money is not a store of value. It is easily manufactured, available in huge quantities and far too cheap to become a source of easily transportable money. Imagine that your entire wealth is in newsprint. When you want to barter that paper for needed goods and services, you would need many truckloads of it.

Therefore, when early societies decided to have gold as a store of value, they knew exactly what they were doing. It was scarce. It is still scarce. It is readily transportable and easily exchanged for goods and services. Today, when we are in real danger of returning to a barter society, albeit a sophisticated one, gold is more important than ever.

Of course, gold's value as real money should not be confused

91

with its utility in making everyday purchases. The currency of the day, issued by the government of the day, will almost certainly remain the primary medium of exchange as long as organized society continues to function. But in times of severe inflation or hyperinflation, currencies will quickly lose their value and a real store of value will be needed.

In Mexico in late 1982 and early 1983, for example, the "value" of the peso deteriorated from 24 pesos per U.S. dollar to 150 pesos per dollar over a period of 2 years. In other words, one day 24,000 pesos would buy U.S. $1,000, but six months later, the same 24,000 pesos would buy only U.S. $130. Of course, the 24,000 pesos also bought much less in Mexico than when their exchange rate against the dollar was stronger. The deterioration has continued, and as this is written the exchange rate is 210 pesos per dollar.

The same thing can happen in the United States or other major Western countries. But if the United States should experience hyperinflation, its impact will be worldwide. U.S. currency can survive Mexican hyperinflation, but no country can survive American hyperinflation.

One thing, one tangible, that will preserve its real value is gold. If you have a physical supply of gold during hyperinflation, you can exchange it for currency and spend that paper the day you get it for whatever you need or want.

We have been taught not to put all our eggs into one basket. In my opinion, however, it makes absolutely no difference whether your eggs break together on the floor of a trust company or separately on the floors of commodity exchanges, banks and savings and loans companies. The important thing is to construct your own basket. If it is strong and well designed, it will hold all your eggs in the days to come.

A few fundamentals have to be understood before we build our sturdy basket. The first is that the currency note that you have in your pocket is not real money, just an IOU between you and the government. By holding that piece of paper in your pocket, you are actually extending a loan to your government, which promises to repay you with real money. At least that used to be the case.

When we had honest governments, all paper currencies were redeemable in gold. Sixty years ago, you could take a piece of paper known as a pound to the Bank of England in London and it would be redeemed for one pound of sterling silver or twelve troy ounces of silver of .925 fineness. Today, they would offer you only two fifty-pence coins or, if you have strong pockets, one hundred pennies. When you take a $100 bill to your government, all you get for it is other bills, more paper but not money.

Those pieces of paper that carry serial numbers are only a product of the printing industry, which the government has found convenient to use in creating an IOU which you pay for through taxes and inflation. If today you can buy one loaf of bread for one piece of paper, and if next year you are asked at the supermarket to pay two pieces of paper for the same or a smaller loaf of bread, the government has actually taken half your money away while you kept the paper securely in your safety deposit box or under your mattress.

Instead of pointing a gun at you and emptying your pocket, the government needs only a handful of armed marshals to guard the printing presses. Eventually, even the size of the notes will become smaller, and they will be printed only on one side to save ink. (The U.S. Treasury Department now uses a photoengraving process to print the reverse of the $1 bill, instead of the hand-engraving process once used. This process allows a 30 percent increase in the volume of larger-denomination bank notes to be printed.) Once we are subjected to runaway inflation, government may even resort to the newspaper presses to keep up with the demand.

Legal counterfeiting by government printing presses is the result of the squandering and deficit spending by the government that we have lived with for the past 50 years. The resulting inflation and currency chaos has made us justifiably distrust our government, along with securities exchanges, trust companies and those lethargic organizations called banks. I do not trust the smiling gentleman who happens to manage my bank account. He and my commodity- and stockbrokers are excellent chaps, and I am on the best of terms with them; but they are not their own masters. Tomorrow morning, the government may close the exchanges or declare a bank holiday. Any morning a new currency may be proclaimed or exchange controls instituted.

No government in the world can forever control the irresistible forces that make a marketplace. Governments usually react, with results that are short-term, very painful and futile. You, who do not have the power to print your own money, cannot afford to react. Those pieces of paper you have stashed away in your mattress or safety deposit box are useless. You have to act, to accumulate something of real value.

Are You Powerless?

Why is it necessary to dig for gold in South Africa and form it into bars and coins in order to bury it again in London, New York or Zurich? The answer is very simple. Gold was and will remain the only reliable scale of material wealth and the policeman of currencies, watching over government printers. Since government has decreed that it may print as much paper as needed to keep the system in power—an act for which you and I would go to jail— the private individual must resort to the only internationally accepted medium to preserve his wealth. He can make sure that his hidden reserve will always reward him with a realistic rate of exchange. The refugees from Vietnam could buy their voyage to liberty only with gold. Some lucky ones were spared Nazi gas chambers or concentration camps by being able to buy their freedom with gold.

Anyone who does not own something develops either a sense of envy or a feeling of self-pity. Both are human nature. So those who do not own gold or make their living out of paper declare that gold is no good. Governments are afraid of gold, because the metal is the gauge of their behavior. If there is no gold in the treasury and if the public believes that gold is a thing of the past, people will not turn in the inked sheets of paper for redemption. So the beautiful merry-go-round turns: as one politician succeeds another, he piles up additional hoards of paper to make his stay in power as comfortable as possible.

The U.S. dollar is the world's premier currency. Its value directly affects some 150 other currencies. When the dollar goes down, there is no lasting refuge, even in the Deutsche mark or the Swiss franc. Those two countries have already tried to discourage gold hoarding through the imposition of various taxes on gold, but the levies had only short-term effects; and once it blew over, people realized that, as usual, the new taxes only heralded additional restraints, which were bound to make gold even more valuable. Gold, even at its high price in excess of $800 an ounce, was still very cheap to the Afghans, Iranians, Poles, Lebanese and other unfortunates caught up in conflicts.

In some of the affluent countries where people still had money, a witch-hunt was directed against Switzerland because of the new tax on gold. This tax could easily be avoided through precious-metal certificates purchased outside Switzerland and redeemable in Switzerland, or purchased in Switzerland and deliverable in London or North America; but most of the experts overlooked this enormous gap in the gold tax law.

There was an uproar in Switzerland against any intervention in the banking and money industry. Accommodating Swiss bankers were sympathetic, particularly to old clients who had suffered from the fluctuations in currencies. The bankers were very keen to fill their coffers with more anxious money, the one service the Swiss have always offered during times of international chaos.

The world was, as always, thriving on fear, and the Swiss turned that fear into a tangible commodity that kept their economy well oiled and operating smoothly. After all, there are approximately one thousand banks in Switzerland compared with fifteen thousand in the United States. On the basis of

Switzerland's percentage of the world population, there should be room in Switzerland for only about half of one bank.

From the dawn of civilization, gold has been the very foundation of society. Gold does not gain in value, the paper IOUs lose in value: the default and stupidity of the rest of the world works for you and gold.

It all boils down to a very simple fact of life: gold is the only easily transportable, easily divisible medium of exchange and real barometer of wealth, and this fact has remained unchanged throughout ancient and modern times.

9
GOLD TO THE YEAR 2000

"Ignorance is degrading when found in company with riches."
—ARTHUR SCHOPENHAUER

We have all been exposed to an explosion of information dealing with the future of gold: unhedged predictions that gold will be up to $5,044 per ounce before 1990, and steadfast predictions that it is going down to $150 per ounce, or less. (Concerning silver, we have heard prophecies of $200 per ounce against bargains to be picked up at $1.50 per ounce.)

An economics professor in the year 2000 might sum up the last two decades of the twentieth century like this: "Never in the history of our study have there been two groups of economists so viciously crusading for their own causes and using cycles and super-cycles to prove that only they were preaching the true gospel."

The speculation mills are in high gear. It is not unusual for half or more of the annually newly mined gold of the entire world—some 700 tons—to be bought and sold on paper by speculators in a single day.

On a certain day in June 1982, a chart line hit another line, and it was declared that gold had hit bottom. Indeed, in the weeks that followed the great buy signal, prices continued upward. Gold climbed to $500, and newsletter publishers were pumping out predictions that the day gold would hit $5,000 was just around the corner.

Then one day, in February 1983, six months after the buy signal, confidence waned for no apparent reason. In 11 trading days, the gold market went into a tailspin and lost more than $100, hovering around $400. In early 1985, it drifted as low as $281.

One cannot escape the feeling that through some process of modern-day alchemy, the roles of astrologers and economists have coalesced to produce a new breed of forecasters. If the magic fortune charts, "proving" that two or three years from now an ounce of gold that cost $300 will reach $5,000, were valid, the world of finance would not be so complicated.

Auri sacra fames, the accursed greed for money, has always lured people into disaster. Nothing was wrong in buying some gold and holding it. But whether gold's highest price will be $500, $1,000, $2,000 or $5,000 per ounce, most of those who rushed to purchase the metal were shoveling cash—usually borrowed cash—at every decline, hoping that it would turn out to be opportunity. Was it only greed, or an almost inherent propensity for financial suicide?

The magic charts, books, newsletter articles and speeches by self-proclaimed "experts" can lead to disaster for the reader or listener. Overwhelmed by the aura of knowledge of the guru, the victims can all too easily be made to swallow a great deal of nonsense.

The might of the media today should not be underestimated. A barrage of words, both written and spoken, has removed most of those involved or interested in precious metals from the basic truth that the fundamentals never alter: only the mood changes. The majority of hard-money gatherings have become the same as media events: mood boutiques, where you can choose the latest trendy idea, tailored to your size and season.

People who have not lost sight of the fundamentals attach little importance to the present price of gold and much more to the future of gold. They are interested in that gold that has been mined since the dawn of civilization and is still around. They have little or no interest in the gold presently being mined or to be mined in the years to come, for this amount is small compared to existing gold supplies.

Between 90,000 and 100,000 tons of gold have been extracted from the earth throughout history, and nature ceased manufacture of the metal some 4 billion years ago. The stockpile aboveground can be increased by, at best, 1 percent per annum. The wise businessman can safely bet that since gold had its bulls and bears in the marketplace 500 years ago and even 5,000 years ago, the metal will be around in the next century or so. Its advocates and detractors have come and gone only to have their places taken by succeeding generations of bulls and bears.

Do you doubt it? Why then does your central bank not sell it off? After all, it is bad business not to take advantage of a price of $300 per ounce if the product is going out of fashion and will be available at $150. Why does your government protect its gold behind steel doors, guarded by armies and tanks? Why keep and protect a parasitic relic?

But governments and central banks are holding onto their gold. Based on data from the International Monetary Fund and the U.S. Bureau of Mines, governmental bodies and central banks in 1980 held over 1,200 million ounces of gold, distributed as follows:

International Monetary Fund	103.43	(million fine troy ounces)
United States	264.32	
West Germany	95.18	
Switzerland	83.28	
France	81.85	
Italy	66.67	
The Netherlands	43.94	
Belgium	34.18	
Japan	24.23	
Canada	20.98	
Great Britain	18.84	
Other IMF Members	113.92	

The rest is held by other countries, such as the Soviet Union, which are not members of the IMF.

On top of the official holdings, it is estimated that private citizens hold between 800 and 1,200 million ounces. Thus, the official estimates of all mined gold is not less than 2 billion ounces and not more than 2.5 billion ounces.

A French Lesson

When we consider private holdings, France immediately springs to mind. Every Frenchman knows that France has in its possession some 5,000 tons of gold, or close to 5 percent of the total gold mined. This figure, of course, does not appear in any official data. But the French have been exploited time and again, and they have learned from their experience that money is not money until it is gold. More sophisticated French citizens say that gold is not gold until it is in a vault in Switzerland. The French may topple a right-wing government and replace it with a left-wing one, but they never change their attitude toward gold. What they know is that whatever money may be, paper is not money and never will be.

Whether it is buried in a vault in Geneva or only under the mattress, the French have never parted with their gold. Kings did not succeed in separating the citizenry from its gold; citizen Robespierre tried and failed; his secret police also tried and failed. President Mitterrand tried to tamper with the real wealth of the French citizen by imposing restrictions on gold and overnight the price of the metal zoomed up by 30 percent in terms of the franc. The shrewdness of the French peasant is deeply rooted in this collective historical experience.

France has the largest gold holding per capita on earth and one would assume, therefore, that it also has the largest gold newsletter industry, but nothing could be further from the truth. You will search in vain to find a French newsletter on hard money or on economic survival strategy, or advertisements for three-day seminars at $1,000 or bargain one-day seminars at

$300. The French have long forgotten more than the sophisticated twentieth-century giants of technology still have to comprehend.

A banker in Paris told me, "You in North America today are at the stage we in Europe were at 500 years ago. The Romans tried to return to the gold standard before us, and so did Genghis Khan. Europeans are no smarter than North Americans; give it another century and your masses too will learn. You simply have to go through the mill."

Learning by Example

When we look at who bought and who sold gold during the last few years, we see that the rich added precious metals to their existing stockpiles. Individuals ought to draw the inevitable conclusion. If the paper yen is that good, why are the banks in Japan going from practically no gold in 1970 to 24 million ounces in 1980, especially when all signs indicate that Japan is still riding a crest of growth and success, while the rest of the world is in decline? In Japan, the sale of Krugerrands and small bars of gold to private individuals has been soaring while we in North America are told to sell our gold because it is going out of fashion. Both the Europeans and the Japanese rely on their intuition.

It is superfluous to dwell on the ambitions of the Communist-bloc inhabitants to own some gold. No doubt those who succeed in leaving Poland these days would much prefer to take the gold coins of the old Poland with them rather than the zlotys of the present regime.

Some "less-developed" countries have opted to retain some of their gold holdings and not sell them, even for food to feed their starving people. In 1980, the Indonesian central bank increased its holdings by 66 tons. Iraq, it is said, is holding back on the sale of its 135 tons of gold and is financing its prolonged war with Iran from other sources. Surely if the government of Iraq was convinced that gold is going down to $150, they would sell their gold to finance their immediate needs and later reacquire the metal at lower prices. Even Israel, which has been plagued with inflation since its establishment, and which "enjoys" triple-digit annual inflation, still holds onto its small quantity of gold.

Evidently, central banks and governments do not believe what we are all advised to believe, namely that the yellow metal is going out of fashion.

Why then do so many people believe the promises of banks, which press on us pieces of paper that we accept as money? Instead we should follow the banks' own unstated policy: we should acquire as much gold as possible, as soon as possible and as cheaply as possible—just as they do.

Instead of being carried away by cyclical declines in price and the supposed losses sustained in gold, we should understand what the headlines are really telling us. The hostages' ransom paid to Iran by the United States in 1981 was done in physical gold. The Iranians would not accept drawing rights or a credit line. Gold was exchanged for humans.

By the middle of the seventeenth century, there were about 500 million people on earth; by the end of the nineteenth century, this number had doubled. By 1970, the figure had swollen to over 3 billion, and by 1980, the world population had reached 4.4 billion. By the year 2000, 6.2 billion people are expected to be roaming the earth.

We have today a total of some 2.5 billion ounces of gold in the world, and its production is increasing only by approximately 1 percent per annum. Two generations ago, should the gold of the world have been distributed among its inhabitants, each person would have received three ounces of gold. Today, a similar exercise would allocate less than three-quarters of an ounce per capita.

The increase in the production of gold is on the decline, and it is anticipated that by the year 2000, only some 500 tons of new gold will become available per annum. In other words, a per capita distribution of gold in the year 2000 will result in less than one-half ounce per citizen of the world.

It does not require a PhD in economics to draw logical conclusions and devise a course of action. An individual should do what his central banks are doing. They have demonstrated nonconfidence in their own receipts and in the paper of their counterparts in other countries time and again. Central bankers believe that we are on the eve of a complete erosion of what is now known as our monetary system.

In the future, gold will become the most sought-after hedge because the present mechanism that has terrorized global monetary standards during the past few decades will collapse.

John Maynard Keynes, the spiritual father of supply-side economics, was once pushed to the wall with questions about how his theory works in the long run. Keynes quipped, "In the end, we are all dead."

Have politicians and the captains of industry adopted the same cynicism? I hope that my readers will not follow them blindly to destruction.

10
GOLD CERTIFICATE SCHEMES

"The golden age only comes to men when they have forgotten gold."
—G. K. CHESTERTON

Whenever I discuss the ownership of gold, I cannot emphasize too strongly that it is essential that you actually possess the gold. In recent years a new trade has developed. Certain trust companies, brokerage houses and banks have managed to get customers on what I call the paper gold bandwagon, based on nontransferable gold certificates.

What are gold certificates? When you purchase a gold certificate from a trust company or brokerage firm, you obtain a piece of paper certifying that it is holding a certain amount of gold for you in its vaults. (Silver certificates work the same way.) In the small print you will find that usually you have to give the trust company adequate notice to obtain physical possession of your gold. People come to my office to redeem a gold certificate issued by someone else. We cannot cash it, of course, and send them back to the institution that issued it. There an unpleasant surprise awaits the certificate holder.

"We are sorry, Mr. Smith," says the bank clerk. "Today we cannot give you the 100 ounces of gold you purchased 18 months ago. We are just out of 100-ounce gold bars."

"Well, the certificate says that I can obtain delivery upon presentation of the certificate," says Mr. Smith. "I would like very much to have my gold today."

The clerk is somewhat distressed, because standing behind Mr. Smith are other people purchasing certificates. So Mr. Smith is bundled into the office of the manager, where he is promised his gold next week. Mr. Smith, like most of the depositors of the bank or trust company, will usually accept that statement and come back next week.

However, if a bank failure is in the works, and we had over 70 in the United States during 1984, Mr. Smith's bank will not give advance notice to the depositors that it intends to close its doors. The bank will close as usual on Friday. On Monday morning, Mr. Smith will find that a bank holiday has been declared. When he arrives at his bank to ask for his gold, he will be unable to get delivery; the IOU in his hand is just an "IOU nothing," another great paper money deception, in which we have been led to believe that worthless paper is valid.

On the day that a bank holiday is declared, thousands of people will converge on the bank, which has been using Mr. Smith's gold certificate deposit to extend mortgage loans to other customers: after all, the bank has to roll over its money. When there is no gold in their vaults, no other forms of money will be available, because banks and trust companies have to maintain only 15 percent liquidity.

Should Mr. Smith succeed in redeeming his gold certificate, turning a piece of paper into a bar of gold, he actually takes bad paper money out of circulation. This impairs the bank's liquidity even further.

If the bank will rent you a box in its own vault where you can deposit your bar of gold, this is fine. I believe that before a raid on safety deposit boxes occurs, a massive default of payment will have to occur, and we should have adequate time to empty the boxes. But you must remain alert: the safety deposit boxes are in the bank, and when the doors are closed, the doors are closed.

Warehouse Receipts: A Riskless Transfer

Some responsible dealers in precious metals are trying to

overcome the problems created by the gold deposit certificates issued by banks and trust companies. Gold warehouse receipts certify that a certain amount of gold or silver has been purchased by you and is available to you or the bearer of the receipt, on demand, during any business day. If this method gains adequate acceptance, we may well experience a return to the honest storage of gold, with less risk than that created by the ambiguous gold certificate schemes.

Warehouse receipts made out to "the bearer" offer an outstanding vehicle for people in restricted economies to own and trade gold and silver. A gentleman from a Middle Eastern country recently purchased a substantial quantity of 100-ounce silver bars. He told the trader serving him that he would be taking the silver to Switzerland and depositing it in a bank there.

He then intended to sell the receipt to an eager purchaser in his country. He was delighted to learn that he did not have to carry silver physically from Canada to Switzerland and possibly subject the silver to a Swiss tax. All he needed was to purchase a warehouse receipt from a Montreal dealer. Ever since, he has been on the road between Montreal and his country of domicile, selling gold and silver in a country where such ownership is prohibited; he is earning a very handsome profit at almost no risk. He did not even have to carry the certificate on his person when he returned to his country.

Any Swiss bank or precious metals dealer in Canada will be willing to confirm to a nonresident the availability of gold and silver that may be stored and delivered upon production of identity or certificates, without any further questions asked.

The Canadian Connection

Today, Canada is an outstanding investment ground for foreigners, who are welcome to open safety deposit boxes or trade in precious metals. (During the First World War, when the Swiss were worried that the Germans might invade their country, Swiss banks transferred a significant portion of their gold holdings to a vault in Montreal.) Canadian customs regulations are quite liberal regarding the moving of bullion in and out of the country: you may declare whatever you bring into Canada without fear of duty. Coin collections and numismatic items are also duty-free. Canada is one of very few countries where you do not have to declare expatriated currency, and, at present, has no exchange controls.

Entrusting your wealth to gold or silver certificates is like giving matches to an arsonist. Gold is the blood, the lifeline, of our economy. Modern industrial society can only function with adequate "blood" in its system. Rather than trusting the Draculas of the central banks, you should have a sufficient supply in your own "blood bank." Anyone offering you a piece of paper for gold or silver, without specifying that you physically own a particular, well-described bar or coin, may be out for your blood. Otherwise, why would he give you paper when he could give you the gold?

11
SILVER—
NO MORE LUSTER?

"Who lined himself with hope,
Eating the air on promise of supply."
—WILLIAM SHAKESPEARE

In June 1984 the U.S. Congress, after years of debate, decided to dispose of its stockpile of silver. The official hoard of $1 billion in silver was slashed to a token $25 million. This is the latest indication that, for a while, the "poor man's gold" is about to become just another commodity, abundantly available and subjected to the mercy of supply and demand forces. Such an occurrence does not spell the end of hard money; it only signals that silver may no longer be a full member of the precious metals family. This situation has been caused by a variety of new elements in the last decade.

We all have vivid memories of the 1979–80 silver bull market: projections of prices of $100 or $200 per ounce sounded plausible during days of increases of $5 per ounce. The world at large was betting on Nelson Bunker Hunt's insatiable appetite. Scenarios of a world shortage of silver triggered by a billion Chinese using instamatic cameras and full-length mirrors were filtered to the press through the self-interest and the naïveté of analysts. A rumor that there was an ever-rising annual world shortage of silver was peddled by hoarders and silver vendors.

In retrospect, there was really nothing special about the 1980 price boom from $10.80 to a high of $48.00 and the subsequent bust. The boom was fueled by greed, attracting buyers who feared either the day after or that they would miss the greatest money-making opportunity in history. They were the reincarnation of those who participated in the tulip escapade of the seventeenth century or who followed John Law in the eighteenth century. The only difference between 1680 and 1980 was that they did not have the Comex and the other electronic wonders we enjoy. Consequently they lost less.

Glut or Shortfall

Since 1979, new mine production and an increase in the mining of copper and other minerals produced millions of ounces of new silver as by-products. The silver shortages, which seemingly plagued the world from 1950 to 1979, became a surplus. That our century actually enjoys an oversupply of silver, when the silver touts offer statistical data that "proves" a shortage, is a bold statement. True, the Western world consumes some 355 million ounces of silver per annum and produces only 250 million ounces. This points to a massive shortfall, traditionally made up from the sales of silverware, old coins and from the never-ending hoards of silver accumulated in India.

Nevertheless, the silver picture started to look negative even during the explosion. During a price orgy, however, few are interested in either reality or bad news. Data compiled by the U.S. Bureau of Mines shows that silver consumption in the United States has declined from 160 million ounces in 1978 to 157 million in 1979, to 124 million in 1980, to 116 million in 1981, to 105 million in 1984. These American statistics mirror those of the entire Western world.

In the immediate future, silver consumption is unlikely to increase. The mirror industry was supposed to boom, yet it has not. In 1976, 4.6 percent of the world's silver went into mirrors; today it is about .5 percent. Moreover, the decline took place while the world population increased by tens of millions.

In addition, through necessity created by rising prices and advances in technology, a variety of substitutes for silver have rendered some 60 percent of traditional uses obsolete during the last few years. The development of digital cameras means that silver imagery is no longer required. The early 8mm and 16mm silver-based films of the home-movie industry have been replaced by a silver-free iron-oxide tape offering instant video images.

Statistics of the annual silver "shortfall" also fail to include the recovery rate of pure silver from scrap, in most instances 90 percent. A silver refinery can be established in a garage corner at a negligible cost. Hundreds of moonlighting refineries have sprung up since 1979. Their output, which runs into millions of ounces, is ignored by the statisticians. (The recovery of metals in general and silver in particular is on the increase. Even aluminum recovery is up from 15 percent in 1972 to some 90 percent in 1985.)

The film and photography industry, which accounts for 45 percent of all annual silver consumption, also contributes to its recovery. A ton of used X-ray film contains approximately $3,000 of silver (at $10 per ounce), and it is very economical to reprocess. Industries using silver are set out in the chart opposite. It is surprising to find that visible products such as jewelry, coins and silverware represent only about 5 percent each of the annual silver market.

Private Investors

During 1980–81, private investors increased their silver holdings by nearly 300 million ounces. It is now estimated that over 1 trillion ounces of refined silver are held by private speculators and individuals, all waiting for and expecting a reoccurrence of 1980, when prices will again move above $50 per ounce. These private investors, who are usually considered to be "weak hands," now have enough silver to supply all the Western world's needs for three years, without an ounce of new silver being mined or recovered from scrap.

It seems that the only factor still holding silver at present price levels is the vested interest of holders of huge hoards, who would

110

like one more profitable opportunity to unload inventories onto a gullible public. Industrial users gladly shift some of their risks to speculators and hope to repurchase silver at prices lower than today's level, perhaps for as little as $4 per ounce or less. When the speculators dump the metal, we should not be surprised to see silver prices tumble to new lows. Once cleaned of its Hunt-inspired tarnished reputation, silver will shine again.

SILVER CONSUMPTION BY END USE

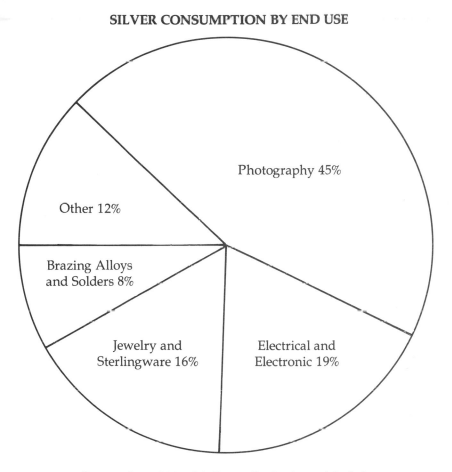

Source: *Annual Metal & Commodity Review and Outlook,*
Rudolf Wolff & Co. Ltd., January 1985

NEW YORK SILVER PRICE 1936–1983

	High	Low	Avg.
1936	49.750¢	44.750¢	45.090¢
1937	46.750¢	44.750¢	44.880¢
1938	44.750¢	42.750¢.	43.230¢
1939	42.750¢	34.750¢	39.080¢
1940	35.625¢	34.750¢	34.770¢
1941	35.125¢	34.750¢	34.780¢
1942	44.750¢	35.125¢	38.330¢
1943	44.750¢	44.750¢	44.750¢
1944	44.750¢	44.750¢	44.750¢
1945	70.750¢	44.750¢	51.930¢
1946	90.125¢	70.750¢	80.150¢
1947	86.250¢	59.750¢	71.820¢
1948	77.500¢	70.000¢	74.360¢
1949	73.250¢	70.000¢	71.930¢
1950	80.000¢	71.750¢	74.170¢
1951	90.160¢	80.000¢	89.370¢
1952	88.000¢	82.750¢	84.940¢
1953	85.250¢	83.250¢	85.190¢
1954	85.250¢	85.250¢	85.250¢
1955	92.000¢	85.250¢	89.100¢
1956	91.625¢	90.000¢	90.830¢
1957	91.375¢	89.625¢	90.820¢
1958	90.375¢	88.625¢	89.040¢
1959	91.625¢	89.875¢	91.200¢
1960	91.375¢	91.375¢	91.375¢
1961	104.750¢	91.375¢	92.450¢
1962	122.000¢	101.250¢	108.521¢
1963	129.300¢	121.000¢	127.912¢
1964	129.300¢	129.300¢	129.300¢
1965	129.300¢	129.300¢	129.300¢
1966	129.300¢	129.300¢	129.300¢
1967	217.000¢	129.300¢	154.967¢
1968	256.500¢	181.000¢	214.460¢
1969	202.500¢	154.000¢	179.067¢
1970	193.000¢	157.200¢	177.084¢
1971	175.200¢	128.800¢	154.564¢
1972	204.800¢	138.700¢	168.455¢
1973	328.000¢	196.200¢	255.756¢

	High	Low	Avg.
1974	670.000¢	327.000¢	470.798¢
1975	522.500¢	391.000¢	441.852¢
1976	510.000¢	381.500¢	435.346¢
1977	496.000¢	432.300¢	462.302¢
1978	629.600¢	482.900¢	540.089¢
1979	2800.000¢	596.100¢	1109.378¢
1980	4800.000¢	1080.000¢	2063.157¢
1981	1645.000¢	795.000¢	1051.837¢
1982	1121.000¢	488.500¢	794.728¢
1983	1466.800¢	837.000¢	1145.339¢

Historic low	24.250¢	12/29/32
Historic high	4800.000¢	1/21/80

Source: Handy-Harman

WORLD SILVER CONSUMPTION
Million Troy Ounces

	1977	1978	1979	1980	1981	1982e	1983e
SUPPLY							
Mine Production							
Mexico	47	51	49	47	53	50	54
Peru	39	37	42	43	47	53	56
Canada	42	41	37	34	36	41	42
United States	38	39	38	32	41	40	41
Other	96	97	103	100	107	113	115
Total	**262**	**265**	**270**	**257**	**284**	**298**	**308**
Secondary Supplies							
Old Scrap	93	82	130	164	125	111	137
Coin Melt	33	21	45	94	18	7	20
South Asian Dishoarding	43	49	41	44	42	37	55
Total	**169**	**152**	**216**	**302**	**185**	**155**	**213**
Other Supply							
Sales from Govt. Stocks	5	9	3	5	4	1	16
Net Exports from Centrally Planned Economies	8	7	14	13	8	0	1
Total	**13**	**16**	**17**	**18**	**12**	**1**	**20**
TOTAL SUPPLY	**444**	**433**	**503**	**577**	**481**	**454**	**538**
FABRICATION DEMAND							
Industrial Demand							
United States	154	160	157	125	117	119	118
Europe	170	173	163	123	119	121	110
Japan	63	65	69	62	60	63	70
Other	70	51	57	53	58	56	57
Total	**457**	**449**	**446**	**363**	**354**	**359**	**355**
Coinage	**35**	**40**	**31**	**15**	**10**	**12**	**16**
TOTAL CONSUMPTION	**492**	**489**	**477**	**378**	**364**	**371**	**371**
CHANGES IN PRIVATE STOCKS	**−48**	**−56**	**26**	**199**	**117**	**83**	**167**
PRICE							
High	$4.98	$6.32	$34.45	$48.70	$16.29	$11.21	$14.72
Low	4.31	4.81	5.92	11.34	7.99	4.98	8.40
Average	4.63	5.41	11.07	20.73	10.50	7.93	11.43

Source: J. Aron Precious Metals Research Group

12
THE UNDERGROUND ECONOMY

"All things are lawful for me,
but all things are not expedient."
—1ST CORINTHIANS 10:23

Has tax dodging replaced soccer or baseball as everyone's national sport? While the legitimate business world is in a recession, the underground economy is flourishing. As the marketplace is becoming more difficult, everyone from homemakers to professionals is becoming involved in the "black" economy. An underground worker can be anyone, from a moonlighter who holds a second, tax-free job to individuals who are illegally employed.

Should you report a neighbor who is running a cottage industry? The teacher who has just tutored your child and requests payment in cash? Did you report all there was to be reported on your last income tax return?

Big government and high taxes have created a subterranean economy that is flourishing in all Western countries. Garage sales and cottage industries are among the "cleanest" tax-evasion operations. The small businessman, the barber or the taxi driver will never report his entire income. Nor do self-employed professionals—lawyers, doctors, shopkeepers, restaurateurs, tradesmen, corporate executives or, of course, multibillion-dollar drug and gambling racketeers.

Tax evasion is probably as old as taxes and tends to intensify when government screws are tightened and the value of its money becomes unstable.

The International Labour Office in Geneva feels that the black market can be beneficial, because it acts as a safety valve, helping to relieve social tension due to the fiscal crisis and unemployment. The Western world is crumbling under the strain of massive financial chaos brought about during the last 40 years by deficit spending. Because of the tremendous underlying economic tensions throughout the world, government efforts to crack down on the underground economy usually fail.

In Rome, 70 percent of all civil servants hold tax-free second jobs. The underground economy boosts Italy's gross national product between 15 to 20 percent, and involves approximately 27 percent of Italy's labor force. When the Communist mayor of Naples tried to crack down on tobacco smuggling, he found out that 60,000 Neapolitans earned their living skirting the state's tobacco monopoly laws. He had to back down.

In France, it is estimated that the *travail noir* work force evaded close to 30 billion francs in taxation during 1978. French governments have tried to suppress the "black labor" since the beginning of the century, but today, with high unemployment and inflation, the quest for additional funds is on. Although public civil servants are not supposed to have second jobs, thousands defy the law. A French tax expert may moonlight as an interior decorator, and Paris firemen are considered excellent plumbers.

The problem is not only restricted to weak economies. In West Germany, which has boasted a strong mark over the past few years, *schwarzarbeit* is flourishing. It is estimated that in 1979, almost DM 30 billion was skimmed off through tax evasion by the underground economy. In Great Britain, Inland Revenue estimates that it lost $8 billion (U.S.) worth of taxes on undeclared income of approximately $32 billion.

In Thailand, there are more people who evade than pay: at least 75 percent of individuals "underestimate" their taxes or don't file at all. Some 53 percent of Thai firms show a loss, and another 38 percent declare profits of $3,600 or less. Smuggling also is essential to Thailand's economy: Cambodian refugees crossing into

Thailand often bring in gold, the only medium of exchange accepted in that war-tormented part of the world. Big buyers are said to purchase thousands of ounces per day. The government does not have the budget to implement thorough controls, and some investigators succumb to bribery or are part of the smuggling network.

The effects of excessive and oppressive taxation are seen in recent events in Sweden, where a recent law made it mandatory for landlords and property owners to report any work done on their property by craftsmen moonlighting from other jobs. Yet the Swedish government was still losing $4 billion (U.S.) per year in taxes to the underground economy.

In the United States, conservative estimates of unpaid taxes start at $200 billion a year. A more realistic estimate puts the amount as high as $400 billion. The underground economy represents between 14 and 30 percent of the U.S. gross national product. (As many as 30 million people in the United States and some 4 million in Canada are tax dodgers.) For example, unlicensed gypsy cabs outnumber New York City's 12,000 licensed cabs by almost four to one. With the number of cab medallions frozen, their price has risen to $60,000 each, so an estimated 40,000 taxi drivers don't bother with licenses or declaring their incomes. The vast majority of gypsy cab drivers are members of minority groups, which are disproportionately represented on the welfare and unemployment rolls. Yet their occupation is illegal, because the government restricts their entry into the taxicab business. Federal, New York State and New York City governments would be much better off legalizing these cab drivers and collecting tax revenues from them.

Also expanding the underground economy are loan sharks and other individuals who do not file tax returns. According to U.S. statistics, narcotics dealers evade up to $8 billion a year in taxes. Investors in securities, real estate, art and livestock routinely conceal their profits. Within the "gray" area of tax dodging are some oil and gas investments in the United States, indigenous Canadian movies and numerous offshore tax shelters. There used to be an attraction in investing in coins and stamps that could easily be bought and sold without the tax man knowing about it; however, many states have already implemented restrictions to close the gaps in numismatics. On the vast continent of North America, tax dodgers can always find a loophole, such as the formation of new churches and the ordination by mail of ministers of religion to obtain tax-exempt status.

Another way to avoid paying taxes is "contra deals" or barter: exchanging one service for another so that no cash changes hands. Medical doctors are trading talents with lawyers, and dentists receive landscaped gardens in exchange for root canal work. Taxation departments maintain that even if no cash changes hands, the value of the goods or services traded should be treated as cash. (This also goes for garage sales!) Tax regulations notwithstanding, such income is rarely if ever reported.

Businessmen use offshore tax havens and financial centers to trade commodities, buy and sell stocks and even invest in their own businesses. Restaurants, dry cleaners, boutiques, and small hotels and motels often underreport their receipts. If every small business reported and paid taxes on every dime of its total receipts, many more would be going bankrupt than the too-large number that are folding now. For many small businesses the "skim" is all that keeps them afloat in times of inflation or recession.

The roots of the underground economy are moral as well as fiscal, an extension of the tax revolt now engulfing the citizenry of the whole Western world. The impetus for tax dodging is no longer the thrill of getting away with it; it is a rebellion of the masses disgusted with government squandering.

Government Intervention

Four hundred billion dollars changing hands underground in the United States alone is too tempting a bait for any administration to bypass. After some time, this cash can be trapped by governments only by changing the color of the bank notes.

It usually happens on a Monday morning. You will know when it is about to happen: the president or the minister of finance will make an appearance on national TV a few days before the impending change. He will unequivocally deny the "malicious rumors" that a currency devaluation or change is in the offing. Politicians and bureaucrats will confiscate undeclared fortunes and create some breathing space for yet another government spending extravaganza.

It is not the drug peddler, smuggler or protection racketeer that the government wants. It is everyone, mainly the prudent, responsible citizens who have been answering the patriotic call to invest in stocks, bonds and other so-called investments. All the old money that has been dipped into various promising ventures other than gold or the cost of living should be considered sunk. The politicians will attempt to devise a new carrot to entice good citizens; they will try to attach new investments to a supposedly more realistic currency in order to restore confidence and get more tax revenues from a gullible public.

A Taxpayer Revolution

The United States Declaration of Independence says that governments derive their just powers from the consent of the governed. A typical, middle-class American pays 40 percent or more of his gross earnings in taxes of one form or another: federal and state income taxes, social security taxes, sales taxes, excise taxes, property taxes and more. Many Americans and like-minded and overtaxed citizens of other countries are withdrawing their consent to being taxed at 40 percent and more of their earnings. They realize that the act of voting does not signify "consent" to all that their elected representatives do in their names, even if every candidate they voted for in the last election happens to have won.

The other day I had an argument with a British investor. He has called for an out-and-out war against big government. He suggested that people should not pay any taxes, because the government is just squandering our money and taking us for a ride. I decided to play the devil's advocate: "What about the taxes to maintain highways, police protection, the fire department and an ambulance service? Your suggestion would bring about a complete collapse of the present system. The system may not be ideal, but whatever will take over may be far more dangerous than what we have now." I added that many tax evaders are wrapping themselves in a cloak of hypocrisy to justify a parasitic way of living. They claim that their great capitalistic ego has been diluted, and so have their accumulated fortunes. I concluded by comparing him to the atheist writer who writes a book and prays for its success.

He agreed that he would be willing to pay part of his taxes, if he knew that they were employed in useful and essential services "needed to maintain a civilized society." He agreed that some system of courts, of law and contract enforcement is needed. He likewise agreed to the need for fire departments and police protection. When I proposed that he should forward $5,000 out of the $10,000 in taxes he should have paid last year on his underground income, he was in a tight corner. He is a loyal British subject and otherwise a law-abiding citizen. I proposed that he dispatch the $5,000 to Inland Revenue anonymously, because if he admitted that he should have paid $10,000, he would subject himself to untold harassment.

We concluded that paying taxes is really a matter of conscience. That is the bottom line that every responsible citizen, in my opinion, should take. If you are unhappy with your politicians or your congressman, you should try to unseat him and make sure that the substitute will be better. If you feel that you can contribute to government service, then join the civil service; but you cannot extract yourself from a system whose protection and benefits you enjoy. I would leave it, therefore, as a matter of conscience when it comes to tax evasion. Tax avoidance, of course, is quite legal, but unfortunately the areas between the two are sometimes gray and obscure, and the problem is as old as humanity.

INVESTMENT AND TRADING

13
THE NEW FLOW OF WEALTH: THE DAY OF THE SWING TRADER

"The masses are asses."
—WINSTON CHURCHILL

The economic gurus of North America and the world, allegedly the brightest and the best, appear each Friday on "Wall Street Week," and periodically on a *Wall Street Journal's BARRON'S* panel, to predict where the various markets are heading. Then the mob follows. After all, the experts must be right or they wouldn't be on television.

When the forecasters' past performances are reviewed, allegedly they all have made 30, 40, 50 percent and more on their investments. However, people overlook the fact that the majority of these forecasters have to make "good" predictions: their professional survival depends on it. Therefore, the smart ones make lots of forecasts and somewhere, somehow, a few of these predictions will be on target.

All these great minds are unequivocally bullish. They know that the general public are good buyers and awful sellers. Since only a "buy" consensus is comforting, they tell the public what they want to hear. Then on Monday morning, after Friday's "Wall Street Week," they rush into a new position. When the news is "good," meaning that the stock market is going to 1,500 this year and commodity prices will explode because of inflation, they want you, the buyer, to forget fundamental practices and be swept into the programmed move.

Who cares that the New York stock market sits on a time bomb of a $21 billion margin debt; if it goes off, it could halve the value of the Dow-Jones Industrial Average (DJIA) and close the stock exchanges. Never before in human memory has there been so much confusion and so many predictions, contradictions, explanations and excuses to be interpreted by the unwary investor.

In the early 1980s the concept of individual and international trading changed when instantaneous money transfers through computer entries became readily available. The physical market, with its classical response to supply and demand, ceased to be the deciding factor of pricing. The activity moved from London's Hatton Garden gold-fixing rooms and the grain bazaars of the world to the commodity pits. Now the tail was wagging the dog. Speculators in commodities became the modern underwriters of world affairs and tangible goods. For a price, tens of thousands of individuals and corporations were and still are willing to buy or sell a risk during every business day. Oil producers along with soybean growers can lock in a profit by undertaking future delivery at today's prices.

Whether Cuba or some other sugar-growing country likes the activity on the North American Commodity Exchanges does not alter the fact that the price of Number Eleven sugar dropped to $.025 a pound in June 1985. Never mind that your grocer still charges $1 a pound for sugar. Do not attempt to understand why it is impossible to produce sugar for $.05 a pound. Don't try to explain why copper is not a bargain at $.64 a pound in May 1984 or at $.57 a pound in November of the same year. The fact remains that buyers and sellers are willing to accept and underwrite the risk of such "ridiculously low" prices.

An imaginative writer can easily develop a scenario for the demise of OPEC through the commodity futures markets. On May 16, 1984, when the Gulf War erupted and a Saudi oil tanker was hit, the price of crude oil on the futures market rocketed by $1 per barrel, representing a 4 percent increase. The volume of trading exceeded 17,000 contracts, in practical terms 17 million barrels of

124

oil. This took place at a time when OPEC's entire production was 14 million barrels per day. In other words, some 120 percent of OPEC's production on that day was changing hands between speculators, the majority of whom had never seen an oil barrel, let alone an oil well or an oil tanker.

Gold Digging

The world gold market is now dominated by the New York and Chicago exchanges. For one hundred years, every morning in London at 10:00 A.M., the entire investment community of the world anxiously looked to five men with their five flags for the gold fix. But in recent years the representatives of the participants in the trading room of the Rothschilds in London have been looking to their wire service screens, waiting for the opening of the New York and Chicago exchanges before making their fix. The daily trading value on the North American Commodity Exchanges exceeds 50 percent of the world annual production of new gold. During some active days, 75 percent or even 100 percent of the annual new gold production may shift hands among speculators on paper. Traders everywhere are now immensely affected by what takes place in the trading pits of New York and Chicago.

In the commodities game, as in many other businesses in the good old days, 85 percent of the players are losers and only 15 percent are winners—about the same odds as horse racing or gambling. Yet the public still flocks to racecourses and the gaming pits.

These odds, however, do not mean that "Little Me" is powerless. Imagine that you are given a very special privilege—to go to the Kentucky Derby and place your bet after two minutes have elapsed of a three-minute race. Your odds now are surely better than those of the average punter. But your odds will improve significantly if you know something about the race itself. The horse in front after two minutes may not necessarily be the winner if he is fast out of the gate but tires in the stretch.

Today commodities markets move at the speed of light. The successful trader does not look just to fundamentals, although they are very important, but is also a master of both his and other people's emotions. He is very aware that we live in a rapidly changing social, political and economic environment. One of the most respected technical analysts of our current era is Robert Prechter, a psychology graduate of Yale University. Prechter is listened to by a hoard of economists and fundamentalists, who can't figure out why their formal education and practical experience have led them to unprofitable ventures in the commodities markets.

Another respected analyst and market observer, André Hudson, has observed that most of today's traders are living in the Wright Brothers' era, not the supersonic age. To trade commodities successfully, Hudson believes, a trader must be able to act before others react. He must have a form of radar—to be able to identify an airplane well before he hears the roar of its engines. One reason 85 percent of commodity traders are unsuccessful is because they react to events, figuratively speaking a sonic boom, and think they are anticipating a trend, when in fact the 15 percent who are winners acted before the other 85 percent heard the noise.

During November 1983, after three tons of gold were stolen from a Brink's depository in London, the price of gold rallied from $375 to $400 per ounce. TV and newspaper headlines speculated that this incident brought about the increase in the price of gold. However, logic shows that such a theory is just silly. There are approximately 100,000 tons of gold on earth, accumulated and hoarded for 5,000 years. Is it possible that three stolen tons, valued at $38 million (at $400 per ounce), could raise the value of all the gold on the earth by $25 per ounce, or $80 billion? No. The robbery triggered the headlines, the mob stormed in and bought, and some very complacent experts were willing to sell gold at $25 more than they could have the day before the Brink's heist.

126

For every buyer there must have been a seller; someone who sold his gold to the eager public at $400 per ounce. The seller did so knowing that after a period of time he would be able to purchase back his gold at a lower price, making a handsome profit. A big eager bear was selling gold to all the little greedy bulls who were hoping that the Brink's robbery would propel them into instantaneous wealth. After three days the price of gold was back down to $377, and the seller was able to buy back his gold for a profit of $23 per ounce—not a bad payoff for a three-day investment in time.

Market history has proven time and again that there are small bears, small bulls and some big bulls, but at the top of the heap there are, in most cases, big bears. The big bear is the one who walks away with the most money. He may not be the smartest, but he owns the largest purse and has the largest belly to stomach the vicious breaks of the market.

In addition to the game of gold played periodically according to the uncertainties and miseries of mankind, the annual orange juice story repeats itself every December and January. When the first cold wave hits Florida, the TV news programs show citrus farmers fighting the frost, warning the viewer that the current crop will be severely damaged if the below-normal temperatures prevail for another day. As surely as God made oranges, the next morning the mob will bid the price of orange juice up to the limit. It will be squeezed up for a day, a week or a month. Then, from $1.80 or $1.90 per pound, the price of orange juice is squeezed down again by $.20 or $.30.

Once more, the stampede has no rationale. The news of a bad crop was already in the market, and very well discounted. A simple truth about orange juice is that once the frost sets in there is more, not less, concentrate. The growers crush oranges around the clock; all the fruit that is slightly frostbitten and cannot be sold as oranges is frozen into concentrate.

A few knowledgeable locals in the orange juice pit and the gold pit made a lot of money following the Brink's robbery and

Florida's latest winter frost. They were there early in the morning. By the time the TV viewer's broker put his order through, the locals in the pit had hyped up the market by another few points to lure in some more greedy bulls who would then sell just before the close of the market for the day. A very comforting roll of $100 bills, plucked off the latest orange freeze, was warming their pockets. Again, the big bears were ready for the amateurs when the newspaper headlines and TV commentators predicted an ever-increasing price of orange juice.

A Modern Bazaar

At this point, our prime objective is to deal with the part-time speculator and full-time dreamer who wants to be successful. This potential investor is likely to be well-educated, knowledge-able about computers and other modern wizardries, and a college graduate living on less than $30,000 per annum. To trade commodities, he will have to open an account with a brokerage firm. This will get him in the door, and enable him to trade from his home or office, whenever the markets are open.

The commodity market is a modern bazaar where one can establish a phantom trading booth in the form of a telephone connection. Contact can be established with the trading pit through an intermediary—a commodity broker. Modern electronics allow the investor to take a position and speculate on current events as they happen around the world. If world affairs do not appeal to you, you can assume a more narrow outlook. Combine fundamental observations with the study of cyclical effects regarding the present price and future moves of grains, precious metals, pork bellies, cocoa or financial futures. For a small commission paid by you and shared among the broker, the clearing house and the exchange, you gain access to the most efficient marketplace on earth, the worldwide, sensitive, modern commodity bazaar.

Armed with a nominal amount of common sense and discipline, you can set up your trading booth as a speculator. By trying to speculate, you still differ a great deal from a gambler. A speculator assumes risks, whereas a gambler creates risks. A speculator runs his own little Lloyds of London. He is an underwriter and, as such, hopes to be rewarded for his anguish, time and money.

To speculate successfully you need discipline, risk capital and imagination. You also need to follow certain precautions—precautions 85 percent of today's commodities traders neglect.

First, know the markets you are trading. If you understand precious metals, you may be able to trade gold, silver and platinum successfully. If you understand the meat business, you may succeed in cattle and pork bellies. If you have a farming background, you may be able to come out ahead in corn, wheat and soybeans. If you have a banking background, have a go at currencies futures. If you have no particular background, learn the fundamentals of any market you decide to enter. Don't just say, "I want to make money in commodities, so I think I'll go long (or short) on gold, lumber or the Swiss franc."

Second, play the commodities markets only with money you can afford to lose. Do not put a mortgage on your house or dip into the funds you have set aside for your children's education. Remember that there are fees and commissions involved, and to break even you have to make a certain amount of profit on your trade. Impatient day traders, who may have a theoretical profit after four hours of trading silver, may in fact have a loss when their transaction costs are included.

Third, control your trades and do not let your trades control you. Have stop-loss points firmly established and take your lumps if the market moves against you. Let your winning trades ride-raise your stop-loss as the market goes up (or down) in your favor. Not every trade you make will be a winning trade, so maximize your profits from your successful trades and minimize your losses from the bad ones.

Shopping for a Broker

I recommend that you deal with a medium-sized firm that specializes in commodities trading, and not a major national or multinational firm that may trade stocks and bonds as well. At the smaller firm you will not just be a computer entry, but a client whose business is valued. You should deal with an experienced broker, and a firm that has been around for at least five years. A firm that has been around for five or more years should know its business, and have retained enough satisfied clients to be assured of continuing in business. All brokerage houses are licensed and bonded, giving the investor protection against negligence or criminal misconduct by an employee of the firm.

Do not look for "bargains," but don't be afraid to shop around for competitive rates. Full-service brokers charge between $60 and $120 for overnight trades (trades that take more than one business day to complete), and between $40 and $80 for day trades (transactions that are opened and closed on the same day). You will soon discover that the major national or multinationals— Merrill Lynch, Richardson Securities, Bache and Shearson, American Express—will charge you the high end of the scale; the smaller firms will generally charge toward the lower end. The higher rates charged by the larger companies are necessary to cover their high overheads: plush offices, major advertising campaigns and administrative staff.

You should, however, avoid the discount broker who operates from an office rather than the trading pits, and the managed accounts touted over the phone and by direct mail. Many of these firms are very thinly capitalized, not properly licensed and regulated, and need a constant infusion of new funds to pay their rent and sales commissions. A mid-sized, full-service brokerage firm offers you charts, research data and current market information as effectively as a much larger firm, and at a lower cost.

All trading in futures is conducted through a margin account. The initial margin required to trade commodity futures is significantly less than that required to trade stocks, often as low as 10 percent of the contract price. Since commodity prices tend to fluctuate much more rapidly than stock prices, the potential for gain, and loss, is much greater than in trading stocks.

130

The Long and Short of It

When it comes to selling short, betting that the price of a commodity will decline, commodity futures offer a definite advantage over stocks. You can sell short as easily as you can go long. You do not need an "uptick," as with stocks. Since most investors are instinctively bullish (thinking in terms of buying and holding), there are often greater opportunities in going short than in going long.

Unfortunately, many brokers are not interested in helping you sell short—they're hoping to keep this lucrative piece of business for themselves. The short-seller is often a professional, well aware of the natural bullish orientation of most investors. When he sells a stock or a commodity short, he hopes to be able to repurchase it for less than the buyer paid him for it, and pocket the difference as his profit.

Stocks and bonds are designed to be bought and held for long periods, sometimes in perpetuity. A commodity futures contract always has a termination date. You can't forget a futures contract in your desk drawer or in your safety deposit box. A daily or weekly conference with your broker gives you the information you need to decide whether to hold your current positions, or take your profits or losses. Your broker sits facing the quote machine from eight to ten hours a day, gathering information on behalf of you and his other clients. That is why you pay him commissions. If your broker doesn't offer you this service, cheerfully and freely, find another broker.

When you buy a stock on margin, you become the owner of the stock, and your broker will charge you interest on the outstanding balance due. Your initial installment is a down payment, and your broker will keep the shares as collateral until you pay off the balance due or sell the shares. Should you sell, the broker will first reimburse himself for the "loan" extended to you, deduct his fees and commissions and only then pay you the balance, if any. In commodity futures, you pay no interest on the difference between the margin and the full price. You do not own the commodity unless and until you pay for it in full. You have the right, but are not obligated, to take physical delivery of your commodity if you are long, or offer the actual goods if you are short. However, since over 99 percent of all commodity market participants never take or make delivery, the time span from instituting a contract to its liquidation, particularly if you are on the right side of the market, is interest-free to the tune of 90 percent of the value of the contract.

The leverage, i.e., the dollar control over an asset in commodities, as compared to stocks, is quite significant. In a stock margin account, both in the United States and Canada, the requirement is about 50 percent. For example, if you wish to buy 1,000 shares of a $10 stock, your broker will demand a deposit of $5,000. Should your stock move from $10 to $12, an advance of 20 percent, you will gross a profit of $2,000 on a deposit of $5,000 or 40 percent ($2,000 ÷ $5,000).

The same $5,000 can be used to buy or to sell 3 contracts of gold (300 ounces). This gives you control or leverage on 300 ounces, say at $300 per ounce, which equals $90,000. The same profit expectation as in our stock example, assuming that gold advances 20 percent to $360 per ounce, will spell a profit of 360 percent (300 × 60 = $18,000 ÷ $5,000). Your margin in gold was 5.5 percent ($5,000 ÷ $90,000) versus 50 percent in stocks.

This is what leverage is all about. Your bank is doing it with your savings account, your government with your tax dollar. You can do it on other people's money as long as it is available for free.

However, be warned. Leverage may cut both ways. Your losses can be spectacular if you do not practice self-discipline, stop losses and good humor.

You will soon find out where you can excel: as a day trader, position trader, hedger, arbitrageur, spreads player, etc. Eventually you will label yourself as a fundamentalist, a technician or a mix of both. The literature that your broker will offer you free of charge will be a basket full of ideas, scenarios, expectations and broken egos. By writing for free strategy newsletters or subscribing for an initial trial run (see Appendix IV), your eyes will be opened to ideas, strategies and recommendations which may sway you one way or the other.

The final decision to take the plunge will be yours alone. Don't forget that all those who write newsletters do so for a fee and if they were all that great ... yes, you guessed it, they would not write newsletters. Most of them would trade according to their magnificent strategies and sip piña coladas under a palm tree.

Profiting from Congestion Zones

The early and mid-1980s have seen many markets with a sideways to downward bias. During such a period, which is characterized by a lack of big-money interest and operates mostly on guess, gall and brokers' tips, the nibbler reigns. Volume is low and there is no clear trend, up or down. The market will be in a congestion area.

A congestion area is a trading zone in which prices zigzag in sideways moves that tend to contain price declines and check price rises. Unfortunately, congestion trading means that the market moves without a discernible price trend. Here is where a "feel" is more important than the ability to chart or to interpret market data.

Today, when the thought and imagination essential to commerce and industry have given way to computers, technical traders are time and again pushed to one side of the trading vessel, convinced that the ship is about to sink. Panic-stricken, they jump from one trading range to the other, to be whipsawed at both ends. More often than not, the modern technical trader pays heavy penalties for engaging in pure computer trading and implementing his "top secret" formula that has been sold to and copied by thousands of other traders.

When prices are in a congestion area, the bottom line is how to achieve relatively large gains while incurring small losses. If you have mastered the principles of this new trading reality, you should be able to profit from many small trades, when prices fluctuate within the congestion area. A few simple strategies can be derived from the following charts:

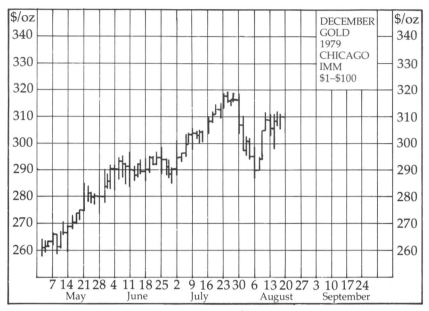

(Chart by Clayton Brokerage Co. of St. Louis)

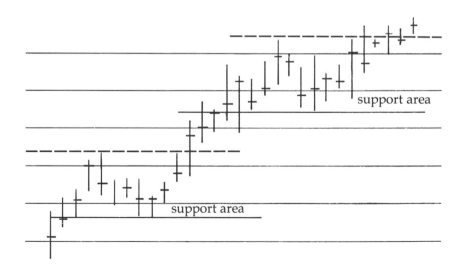

support area

support area

(Chart by the Chicago Board of Trade)

134

Trading in a congested area could be compared to being stuck in a muddy field between two highways in your car. With the aid of chains, you advance inch by inch and count your blessings. It is an unemotional strategy which can pay handsomely if applied with discipline. Admittedly, it is not the most pleasant way of trading futures, but as long as you are not on the highway of a move, trading between congestion lines is about the only profitable method.

Playing the Ratios and Spreads

Many traders follow the gold and silver ratio, playing it either from the extremes or within trading ranges. The last few years have been relatively dull in market moves for precious metals. But ratios are profitable even in almost flat markets.

A recent historic low in the gold and silver ratio was about 1:16, meaning that 1 ounce of gold purchased 16 ounces of silver, or that only 16 ounces of silver were needed to acquire 1 ounce of gold. During January 1980, when precious metals exploded for a brief moment, the ratio was about 1:17 (gold $850 ÷ silver $50 = 17). Immediately after going to one extreme, silver plummeted, and in June 1982 the ratio reached 1:62. In other words, 1 ounce of gold purchased 62 ounces of silver when gold was $297 and silver under $5. Disregarding the extremes, which do not occur on an everyday basis, a very realistic ratio for the foreseeable future, would be from 1:32 to 1:35. I selected this ratio because it is easy to follow for a practical exercise of trading 1 kilo of gold (32.15 ounces) versus 1,000 ounces of silver. This ratio works well both for the conservative who wishes to remain in the physical markets and the speculator who wishes to use the futures market. The following practical example should demonstrate the use of this ratio.

On September 12, 1983, the price of gold was $414.15 U.S.; the price of silver was $12.17, based on a New York closing, a ratio of 1:34.03. If you sold 1,000 ounces of silver and bought 1 kilo of gold on that day, you would have obtained the following results:

September 12, 1983		*May 7, 1984*	
Sold 1,000 oz silver	$12,170	Bought 1,000 oz silver	$ 8,610
Bought 1 kilo gold	$13,314	Sold 1 kilo gold	$11,957

CHANGE:	Silver (profit)	$3,560
	Gold (loss)	$1,357
	NET PROFIT	$2,203

This is a conservative spread implemented with 100 percent funding in physical metals. The return on capital is quite significant. The entire transaction was done within the world of precious metals. Should the same spread have been instituted through the futures market, the nominal margin of a few hundred dollars would have turned into a huge, if not extraordinary, return on capital.

Some speculators act with much larger positions; being well hedged gives them the necessary confidence to take full advantage of the disparities between the two precious metals. They keep on increasing their weight whenever the ratio between the two metals swings to their advantage. They calculate profits in ounces, not in dollars.

Don't be put off too easily. You may have more losing trades than winning trades and still come out ahead if you can ride your winners and cut your losses. Discipline and perseverance are essential for a successful commodities trader.

It is important that you trade in a liquid market that has a substantial volume and a large open interest, meaning that the net unsold or unbought contracts are there in large volume. Most major newspapers carry a detailed commodities section, which includes open interest and volume. You will be well served by reading *Barron's* excellent commodities section on the weekend. It will give you important information on the highs and lows for the week, as well as seasonal information.

You don't need to be extremely wealthy, play ratios or follow a computer system to be a successful commodities trader. Success can come to intelligent amateurs who have shown skill and good judgment.

I know of an oil company executive who retired comfortably at the age of 60. His pension and defensive investments over a period of almost 40 years gave him enough income to maintain his usual standard of living. However, a sudden vacuum was created in his life when he left the pressures and intrigues of his multinational company. Going from a ten-hour day and frequent business trips to visiting the library and playing with his grandchildren was too drastic a change. In the absence of a hobby, our former executive felt that he was fading away. He needed some action.

Three years ago, our oil executive allocated $10,000—which he could afford to lose—to trading commodities. He says, "Every morning I spend 90 minutes in my 'office,' reading the *Wall Street Journal* and the local newspapers. Then, between 8:30 and 9:00, I chat with my broker. Sometimes I take a position and sometimes I don't. Then I get on with my daily routine." It seems that, in this case anyway, commodity trading was a real cure for premature aging.

One reason commodity trading was such a boon to this retired executive is that he was a consistent winner. His commodity account covered his vacations, bought his Romeo y Juliet cigars and presents for his grandchildren. As a senior executive, he was used to first-class travel, and he now spends four months a year vacationing in Spain or Morocco.

My friend is a winner because he does three things that most other people do not do. First, he started with an amount that he could afford to lose. Had he lost his initial stake, he would not have thrown good money after bad. Second, he traded commodities he understood. As a result of his business experience, he had a detailed knowledge of the petroleum and currencies markets, and it is in these areas he made his trades. He never overtraded, or reached beyond his grasp. He did not trade commodities whose fundamentals he was not well versed in. Third, he is disciplined. If a trade goes against him, he cuts his losses. If a trade goes his way, he lets it ride, at least until the trend reverses.

He admits that the market is always right and that he is occasionally wrong. When the market does not act as he anticipates, he takes his losses and sometimes stands aside for days. He never has a margin call, because now he trades with no more than 20 percent of his accumulated equity, with 80 percent kept in T-bills (a U.S. Treasury note), on which the U.S. government pays him 10 percent, more or less, for helping to finance their profligacy.

Eighty percent of his winning trades in 1983 and 1984 were short sales. He did not believe that the price of crude oil would keep rising, or that the dollar would collapse, during that period. "I leave those observations to the prophets of doom, like yourself," he told me with a twinkle in his eye, just after returning from six weeks in Spain. He sold the Swiss franc when two francs bought one dollar, and took hefty profits in currencies and heating oil.

You may possess two out of three of the necessary qualities to be a successful trader. Until you find your way, you can trade contracts of as little as one kilogram of gold on the Mid-American Exchange, or trade a minicontract in grains or financial instruments. Sooner or later, you should develop an affinity for one or more of the 50 commodities and financial instruments traded, and you should be pleasantly surprised at your proficiency. However, if you keep losing, stop trading. Commodities are not, in the final analysis, for everyone.

As the respected financial commentator Verne Myers observed recently, "Today it looks like this device [money] which worked so well is out of whack." It appears that forces beyond our control, like the laws of nature, have gathered enough strength to cause a revolution. The revolution means that investors will have to look to trading, rather than buying and holding investing, to prosper during the remaining years of the twentieth century.

Do not let the recent strength of the U.S. dollar cause you to doubt the truth of Myers's observation. Virtually every other currency has deteriorated vis-à-vis the dollar, and there is still inflation in the United States. The dollar is only relatively strong, not absolutely. As this is written, the U.S. dollar is at the peak of a very mature bull market. As it begins its inevitable decline against other currencies and commodities, persons now profitably holding dollars will seek more profitable investment and trading opportunities. This, I feel, will create a renewed interest in alternative investments, particularly the trading of commodities.

14
THE CLOUDED
CRYSTAL BALL

"The minority is always wrong—at the beginning."
—HERBERT V. PROCHNOW

Rarely in the last three decades have we witnessed such extremes in the marketplace and so much disparity of opinion about the future. Some forecasts predict rampant inflation; others foresee an even more severe recession with cash the king and gold at $150 or less. Heady optimism and grim warnings of collapse, recessions and recoveries succeed one another at an ever-faster pace. The Dow-Jones Average is going up and up. At the same time, some forecasters warn that government deficit spending will bring monetary collapse and that stock prices must crash when public faith in the system inevitably falters. In such times of confusion and conflicting advice, huge fortunes can be made—and lost—in any number of ways. The wise investor will consider all his options—and tread carefully.

One clear warning signal for the future is the number of failures of financial institutions in the United States, which are at their highest level since 1933. This is not supposed to be happening. However, the failure of two large banks today could involve more money than the thousands of small banks that went under during the Great Depression. The FDIC promises to reimburse depositors up to $100,000 of their money as long as funds last, but it has only $12 billion on hand. In the event of a massive failure, depositors will be lucky to receive five cents or ten cents on the dollar from the FDIC.

Even if we accept the ultraconservative figure that bank deposits in the United States are now only $1 trillion, a bailout by the FDIC in the event of a banking collapse will amount to just 1.2 percent of deposits. In addition, the independent agency's funding is made up almost entirely of federal debt certificates. Approximately 80 percent of FDIC assets are made up of government securities, which will have little real purchasing power in the event of a crisis.

Some stockbrokerage houses are also in trouble. Witness the 1982 Cities Service/Gulf Oil takeover attempt in the United States. Large stockbrokerage houses speculated in the stocks. Had the market gone in the anticipated direction and had Gulf honored its takeover offer, the shares would have shot up to $60. However, minutes after Gulf backed out, a hectic sell-off ensued; the shares dropped below $30. Collins, a small firm that bought 1 million shares of Cities Service, went belly-up after it became known that Gulf was opting out. Other large firms were also involved. A potential killing turned into a slaughter of $30 million almost overnight.

Stockbrokers are less regulated than the high-loss commodities industry. In stocks there are no limits on the downside or the upside. If an investor happens to be on the wrong side, only the bell can save him.

It borders on black humor that some stockbrokers who made it up in the investment society by moving from the boiler rooms to oak-paneled offices are now being subjected, but on a much larger scale, to techniques similar to those they used during their struggle to the top. Brokerage houses themselves have been the objects of takeovers, which reached their zenith in 1981. Successful credit card operators bid hotly for brokerage houses, but soon after the takeovers the profits of the plastic cards melted when the newly acquired assets proved to be losing operations.

Negotiated commissions are the death knell of the full-price broker, as the investor who makes his own investment decisions now can go to a discount broker and be served at a fraction of the cost.

The End of an Era

The giant banks are crumbling, and the large stock reptiles must follow. Once the financial dinosaurs disappear, the small, private, conservative banker who knows his clients and their ancestors will have his hands full, and so will small-scale financial advisors and brokers. Files will be dealt with by name again and not by 14-digit computer references. The "backward" operators who did not become involved in the financial supermarkets and one-stop investment centers will be the ones remaining in demand.

While a floundering Western economy, unsound banking practices and an erratic economic recovery dominate the daily news, and savings are brutally smashed on the rocks of inflation, the era of long-term investment is over. The "willing" of shares to widows and grandchildren is past history. Certain investments, however, can still be rewarding. At times like today, the speculator—the individual involved in constant trading—historically has been the most rewarded party. Substantial profits still can be made in the world of supply and demand, known colloquially as "futures."

With a relatively small placement, an individual can take a position and trade in the worldwide marketplace. You can sell Mexican pesos if you know or speculate that the regime is rotten. Capitalize on their further economic failures. Buy Brazilian coffee if you know that a recent freeze can only cause prices to rise. Logically conclude what riots in the mines of South Africa will do to the price of gold. Speculate on what an $8 billion Canadian ego trip to bail out Dome Petroleum will do to the Canadian dollar and to the Canadian banks. There is hardly a single aspect of our daily life, economic or political, that does not influence or affect the marketplace.

The age of the "futures market" is as old as the first human community on our planet with more than two inhabitants willing to barter talents and goods. Some 1,500 years ago China had an organized futures market, which was introduced to Europe by returning explorers. The desire to acquire an ever-increasing variety of goods through trade was a driving force in bringing Europe from the Dark Ages into the economic expansion of the fourteenth and fifteenth centuries. Discoveries of new worlds with new goods to trade for brought ever-increasing desires nourished by the greed that was later transformed into colonialism.

The relics of that colonialism are now known as the Third World. The creation of new countries, which print money and flags faster than maps and encyclopedias can be changed, adds sales booths in the bazaar but does not alter trading fundamentals. Instead of Belgium directly selling African copper, it is now sold through an agent called Zaire, which nevertheless still sells it, via Brussels and London; but you can trade copper without even knowing where Zaire is. The foundations of the metal trade will always remain supply and demand. Fast-buck chartists will try to make a living out of their impressive embellishment of the latest political gossip, but they will not change the basics of the copper market. At the end of the day, it is naively simple: price and its movement depend solely on supply and demand. Your making a killing or taking a licking in copper depends on the time you bought or sold the metal.

Successful trading in futures requires knowledge about the many factors involved in supply and demand. This is not a field for casual investors, which is why some financial writers have given futures a bad name. Many media participants, usually with syndicated wisdom, thought that they could put a little money in the futures market and win a casual trade that would finance a trip to Las Vegas. They considered the trading pits as no more than an extension of Las Vegas; with this attitude they had the usual casino odds stacked against them. Once they lost, and most of them took a beating, they developed an animosity typical of losers. Such reformed and frustrated marketplace crapshooters make bad investment advisors. Writers forget that trading futures preceded the art of reading by thousands of years.

Everyone is involved in "futures," some unknowingly. Farmers, mine operators and manufacturers sell their product in advance against deposits or letters of credit extended to them. The more sophisticated, knowing how markets can fluctuate, hedge their profits. A farmer who sold a million bushels of wheat for December delivery can, at the time of sale, buy a million bushels and minimize the Good Lord's involvement in producing a good crop, in case God has priorities other than providing rain in time, preventing brushfires and watching out for early morning frosts on a few square miles of prairie farmland.

And of course, there are those millions of spectators who watch the daily commercial tug of war. They may have an immediate interest as hedgers, but the majority are like you and me, the audience. In the royal boxes and orchestra seats sit the elite, the seasoned, groomed speculators. The galleries and balconies are occupied by gamblers looking through telescopes. Rarely does a gambler move to the front row, but often a frontrunner loses his nerve and finds his head where his heart is: in the gallery of gamblers.

The tremendous tidal waves that rise and fall in the marketplace discourage most people from taking the plunge. To be discouraged, all you have to do is visit one of the trading pits in New York or Chicago and observe the screams of the "local" or floor brokers. You will quickly conclude that that "crazy work" is not for you. Nevertheless, back in the last decade, many members of the audience *did* get involved in the "crazy work" of the futures market.

One of the cardinal rules of trading commodity futures is never to go on vacation with an open position. Some experts even say that you should never go on vacation near a telephone if you have any positions in the market. This advice would certainly have been well heeded by anyone who left for vacation on June 17, 1982. On that morning, when the spot market of gold penetrated $297 U.S. per ounce, the investment apostles decreed "sell everything," and the public followed. When the selling orgy ended, the public as usual was left holding the bag.

On that day, certain "experts" who had theretofore been staunch supporters of gold advised their readership that "this is it": gold is destined to go to $100 and below, and King Dollar will reign for the rest of our lives. One newsletter writer, famous for being a long-time goldbug, gave his major sell signal almost exactly at the bottom.

The Hunt brothers once more haunted the marketplace. Newsletters fueled rumors that the brothers were sellers this time. In March 1985, the CFTC decided to press charges against them, for alleged manipulations in 1980. Relative to silver, gold was holding well. The "sell everything" mania did not seem to affect the yellow metal as much as silver, whose ratio to gold plummeted to 1:61. A story appeared in one of the newsletters, supported by an "exclusive interview" granted by an "international expert" who was reached in his Bermuda lair, confirming that we were heading for yet a further break which would send the ratio as low as 1:70. June 1982 was the mirror image of January 1980. Whoever was then buying silver at $45 per ounce because "it is going to $200—Howard and Jim said so"—was now selling it.

Commodity brokers had a field day. Taxi drivers and receptionists formed investment clubs. The talk of the town was no longer the hardships inflicted by recession and unemployment. Instead, the favorite topics were pork bellies, sugar, copper and silver, which had reached new lows and surely were going to decline further on Monday morning.

Esoteric formulas, usually reserved for select clientele of fancy advisors booking hourly rates of $600 and more, became headlines. Everyone turned into a contrarian and touted new get-rich formulas. The intensity of public interest in commodities was well reflected on one of the taped information services of a bullion dealer in Montreal, where the number of calls rose from an average of 1,500 per day to 3,000.

The selling pressure of June 17 and 18, 1982, was so intense that margins for certain commodities, such as heating oil, were raised from $2 to $4 thousand, and then from $4 to $8 thousand per contract in a matter of hours. Speculators, or rather gamblers, could only liquidate positions or put up additional margins, which spoiled the fun of going to the casino.

The trouble was that since 1980 the commodity futures market had gained popularity at such a pace that the public was running out of cash. This time many small speculators were selling gold, silver, copper and Canadian dollars that they did not own. They resorted to gambling in futures. Two days of a major trend reversal blew them out of the water, leaving behind their lost margins.

The selling orgy was like a Hollywood set of a casino on fire. When the make-believe flames were out, the professionals who had manipulated the scene must have congratulated themselves on its success.

In June 1982, the mob played into the hands of the commercial dealers again. This time it was the reverse of what happened in January 1980. At that time, the professional dealers were the sellers and "adjusted" the rules of the exchange when the market was overbought by the masses. This time the professionals were the buyers in an oversold market to an extent unknown in recent history. The result was that mid-June 1982 heralded the beginning of a bull move that students may one day use as the textbook for market behavior.

Stocks in 1982–83 mirrored gold and silver in 1979–80. On February 24, 1983, when the Dow-Jones Industrial Average broke above 1,100 it, of course, made headlines on evening news on TV. The sages agreed that the doom and gloom industry really had taken it on the chin; the only way that our "recovery" could go was up, and up was the word. Even busy President Reagan was available for a quick photo session, and for those who still had some doubts, he declared that spring had arrived. The fact that people were still shoveling snow when spring was decreed, and that the following April was one of the coldest and wettest on record, even though the Dow reached 1,226 that month, mattered little.

The very next item on the same newscast was that Dunn and Bradstreet had just announced that business failures for February

1983 were the highest on record, exceeding those of 1932. This did not prevent President Reagan or his secretary of the treasury —who once ran Merrill Lynch, the largest brokerage firm in the United States—from assuring the investing public that the basic reasons for buying stock were still and would remain valid. Buy today, they said, because tomorrow someone else will stampede to bid your shares up adequately to enable you to make a profit. How happy life would be if it were really that uncomplicated.

The trouble is that balloons always burst. But the investing public knows that this soaring experience has to come to some end. The nefarious scheme cannot go on forever. Anyone who goes to a restaurant knows that after his meal he will be handed the bill, and the bottom line is whether the enjoyment was worth the price. In this respect we are referring to ordinary people, not to masochists. Brokers and corporations whose stock has been overbought may still be partying, while the masses who trusted that recovery was around the corner have the hangover that follows a great celebration.

We're Gonna Turn the Bull Loose

In March 1985, Ronald Wilson Reagan became the first U.S. president to visit the New York Stock Exchange. As *Barron's* put it, "He came fully armed with forecasts of happy times. We're gonna turn the bull loose, he vowed to cheering traders." Well, even on the day of the historical visit, prices on the big board closed down. It seemed that the Great Communicator's stock was running out. The last president to make bullish forecasts had been Herbert Hoover in 1929. How good Reagan's ever-green predictions are should be left, with Hoover's, for history to judge.

I hope that readers of this book can avoid the hangover following the celebration by being more informed than the average man in the street concerning the essentials of the stock market. For the benefit of those who do not want to do research, here are some facts. To the majority of people, the Dow-Jones Industrial Average represents the market, and the first question they ask their broker is, "Where is the Dow?" In view of the fact that the majority of investors have never heard about selling a stock or "put" options, the satisfying answer that the market, namely the Dow, is up just confirms that the recovery has started and is going to stay with us.

The fact is, however, that the Dow-Jones Industrial Average represents only 30 of the major U.S. corporations listed on the New York Stock Exchange. The average is computed when the price per share of the 30 stocks is added up and divided by 1,359. Even that figure is not completely accurate, because currently more than 1,500 stocks are trading on the exchange.

The following list shows the names of companies, otherwise known as "blue chip" corporations, who participate in the Dow Average.

THE THIRTY STOCKS IN THE DOW-JONES AVERAGE

Allied Corporation	General Electric	Owens-Illinois
Alcoa	General Foods	Procter and Gamble
American Brands	General Motors	Sears, Roebuck
American Can	Goodyear	Standard Oil of
American Express	Inco	California
American Telephone	International Business	Texaco
and Telegraph	Machines	Union Carbide
Bethlehem Steel	International Harvester	U.S. Steel
Du Pont	International Paper	United Technologies
Eastman Kodak	Merck	Westinghouse Electric
Exxon	Minnesota Mining	F.W. Woolworth

To be accepted into the blue chip club, a corporation must demonstrate growth and consistent dividend payments. Every now and then a corporation is replaced because its horrible record may distort the average. On August 30, 1982, Johns-Manville, which filed for bankruptcy, was replaced by American Express. Earlier in 1981, IBM and Merck were added. Chrysler Corporation was dropped in 1980. Only two companies have been listed consistently for 86 years: General Electric and American Tobacco, presently known as American Brands.

The Dow's restricted corporations has turned this group of stocks into the favorite investment arena for money managers, banking institutions and administration-inspired investors. While it is difficult to manipulate all 30 Dow stocks because of the huge volume traded, critics of the Average maintain that it is easy to influence the Average for a short while by directing huge amounts of money into certain stocks. In 1983, for example, all speculators had to watch was IBM. The moment the shares dropped below $100, it was a fair signal for day traders to take their profits and run or establish short positions, because IBM was usually showing the way for other stocks.

The Dow-Jones Industrial Average is mysteriously worshiped by commentators, economists and television announcers; it is cherished by politicians and bankers who know how to exploit it. The public usually asks, why study market behavior, if the Dow-Jones, which represents only 23 percent of the NYSE, stands for "the market"?

The influence of the Dow on stocks, as demonstrated in February 1983, may last for a while, but in the long run the Dow is far less accurate than the much broader-based Standard and Poor average, which deals with 500 stocks of the New York Stock Exchange and incorporates the famous 30 Dow stocks. The highly sensitive S and P average runs well ahead of the Dow in accuracy, and those who master it can capitalize on it handsomely. Other less publicized measures and indices are: The Wilshire 5000 Equity Index, Pulse of Industry and Trade, Monthly Economic and Financial Indicators, and New Highs and Lows, to mention just a few. Even Sotheby's Art Index has informational value. However, don't ever dream of selling at their publicized prices. According to this index, you will find it most difficult to see prices ever drop.

Keep 'Em Guessing

It is quite obvious why stock brokerage firms, who hold the largest chunk of public money in North America, are opposed to the commodity markets in general and S and P index trading in particular. The good old-fashioned custom of investing in a stock is like offering a hot-air balloon trip to the moon.

Stockbrokers don't like the idea that the public may invest only $6,000 in margin and be able to trade $70,000 worth of stock without the agony of studying the stock, let alone the hot tips of barbers, boiler room operators and newsletter writers. Stockbrokers may even call trading the S and P somewhat unpatriotic: after all, you are betting with or against the performance of a whole market instead of pouring your hard-earned dollars into investments you believe will produce dividends, profits and higher share prices. You no longer look forward to finding someone to offload your shares on for a higher price than you paid. And what about the commissions lost to your broker? That's really un-American.

Stockbrokers and commodity traders want to keep the public guessing. Market analysts and newsletter editors are frequently wrong in their predictions. Goldbugs come and go. Banks fail and governments pretend that their spending sprees will bring economic recovery. Charlatans come and go, leaving behind bemused and often confused followers. Is there anyone we can trust?

The only true observer is history, warning us to beware the mob reaction. Only a relatively few professionals will make their fortunes in stocks and futures, and their gains will come at the expense of a gullible public blindly following every new market trend. The educated investor will avoid the stampede. He will remember that even at $300 per ounce in 1982, gold commanded a value eight times higher than the dollar compared to just a decade earlier. Even grossly oversold and undervalued silver was, in 1982, 500 percent more valuable in terms of the dollar than it was a decade ago.

The years 1980 to 1985 demonstrated that the times for investment in the broad sense of the word are over, at least for years. Take your profits and run is the rule of the new breed of stock market mandarins, T. Boone Pickens and his like. Plan a "green mail raid," hold to ransom a large corporation and rest assured that those at the top will throw millions of dollars at you to call off the proposed takeover.

The parasitical and odious buccaneering of corporations in 1984 and 1985, with self-proclaimed Robin Hoods ostensibly motivated by a need to mend the fences of corporate America, were ominous signs of the times.

In the absence of a philosophy and long-term planning, in an era where confused, microchipped mobs run in all directions, only short-term speculators survive. In cahoots with the Wall Street's raiders of 1985, some money could be made; but being protected by sharks is usually dangerous.

We cannot control or predict the future of the world, but we can find some comfort in the historical truth that gold and silver can be neither massacred one spring morning by the stroke of a pen nor created or decreed at will. While governments and banks continue to tend to lingering problems with short-sighted solutions, and while professional brokers are playing with the crowds who follow them, the wise investor is standing firm and holding onto his insurance in precious metals.

15
THE BEST RECOVERY
MONEY COULD BUY

"C'est pire qu'un crime, c'est une foute."
"It is worse than a crime, it is a blunder."
—ANTOINE BOULAY DE LA MEURTHE

The years 1982, 1983 and 1984 saw only winners in the stock market; when a tidal wave of speculative enthusiasm ensued, it was difficult to tell the public that parabolic price rises are always followed by a smash. My recent business travels, which took me almost halfway around the globe, proved to me that the investing public is afraid of being awakened from the dream that started in August 1982.

The bull market of 1982–1984 has produced over $1 trillion of paper profits on the American exchanges. Newspapers and magazines have been awash with success stories. Harvard University's investment pool has moved upward from $580 million to $2.3 billion since July 1982. The president of the university's management company stated that it was the pool's largest dollar increase in the last 15 years.

The Bronfman brothers, who control 39 percent of Seagrams, saw their paper profits soar by $616 million. IBM's 726,000 shareholders saw the value of each of their shares rocket from $57.50 to $120, for a cumulative gain of $32 billion.

On other stock exchanges, exploding indexes since last year's low paint a picture of endless prosperity. In Sweden, the Stockholm exchange had to close to cope with the barrage of buying. Hectic buying caused an overload, which in turn dictated the shutdown. The only other time in the exchange's history that a prolonged shutdown occurred was in 1930. At that time it was because of the selling.

Some Western countries have put on a much better show than the U.S. performance. Topping the list is Belgium, whose stock exchange by May 1983 was about 75 percent up on its 1982 lows. Eight other industrial nations were not far off in their increases:

Belgium	74.4%	West Germany	40.2%
Netherlands	62.7%	Switzerland	32.6%
Canada	58.5%	Australia	29.7%
Britain	50.8%	Japan	26.9%
France	44.4%		

On both sides of the Atlantic, brokers and financial institutions involved in the daily activities of the stock exchanges had one common "complaint." An Antwerp entrepreneur, who moved from diamonds to stocks three years ago, summed it up, "I have never seen so much money made over such a short period of time. I find it difficult to handle the business coming my way these days."

When asked about what he was doing with his newly made fortunes, he muttered, "Buying!" And as if to justify his decision, he shoved an American newspaper my way. Its headline left no room for doubt: "Billions are being made by investors in a windfall that shows few signs of ending soon." Our Belgian friend, who saw his money tripling and quadrupling, reflects the global frame of mind in this piece of practical wisdom: "Prices go down only if people do not buy" (how true!) "and our psychological makeup commands us to purchase only in a rising market."

"And how long do you think the market will continue to rise?" I asked my friend.

He pointed to another newspaper and underlined: "A windfall that shows few signs of ending soon." He added, "We are safe until the next elections in the United States, in 1988. I have still one hell of a good time ahead of me, and I would be awfully stupid not to cash in on it."

With a bullish consensus of over 90 percent, it is difficult even to attempt a rational evaluation of the situation. It is futile to speak about a parabolic peak of the Dow-Jones Average when the investing public has already been primed to believe that any decline will just pose a buying opportunity. Any argument against such "practical wisdom" would simply limit the conversation.

I tried to reason with a senior banker in Geneva by proposing that the enormous stock holdings he holds for clients should at least be hedged and insured through one of the available instruments, such as the Standard and Poor Contract. He briefly raised his eyes, which were dancing between the *Financial Times*, the *International Herald Tribune* and the two monitors placed on his desk. Smiling from the corner of his mouth in what seemed to be a mixture of pity and self-assurance, he said, "Experts, economists and analysts can be convincing. Frankly, I am afraid to listen to your arguments, which make sense. I am scared that you will convince me to change course. I believe that we are in the midst of a tremendous boom which will carry on for years to come. All the possible corrections have already taken place. Prosperity is likely to continue tomorrow and for another few years." He concluded in a whisper, "Until I vacate this chair to a successor."

In Paris and London things were not very much different than in Belgium and Geneva. The French were joking about a gold coin named "Un Mitterrand": a socialist gold coin guaranteed to always be worth exactly the same. The Mitterrand gold coin will not be made of that terrible metal called gold, which is manipulated by the unscrupulous bankers. It will be made entirely of worthless metal, and therefore it cannot be exploited, it cannot shrink, it cannot grow—and you do not care if you lose it. *Formidable, non?*

Although the French lack faith in their government, the *petite bourgeoisie* has been quite happy reaping the benefits of the Paris *bourse*, which in the last few months has posted an increase of some 45 percent. The market euphoria that swept France in May 1983 engulfed almost everyone. An academic who until a few months ago would not touch the stock market with a ten-foot pole because, as he told me years ago, "I do not invest in anything which I do not understand," could not forgo the temptation and plunged into stock. He would have been better off resisting temptation and restricting his financial pleasures to the one suggested by Voltaire, who got his practical education amongst the cold and boring Swiss bankers: "I advise you to go on living solely to enrage those who are paying your annuities. It is the only pleasure I have left."

In London, the situation was basically the same, with one exception; Joe Granville is more popular in England than in France. When I mentioned that the charismatic American commentator had recommended, during the past few months, that his clients stay on the sidelines and that the aggressive ones sell short, a London investment advisor who also frequents North America shrugged his shoulders.

"I am one of the few who reads the *Granville Market Letter*. That guy has not stopped amusing me for the past year." With a somewhat more guarded tone he added, "Possibly he is right, but I cannot make any money from being right long-term. Even if we have to draw a line between investment and investment dreams, my money is presently on dreams."

The dream must eventually come to an end. As an Egyptian economist quipped, "*Inshallah!* So far we were lucky; now we need a miracle." Neither economists nor the media will provide the answer when we wake up to find that the current investment "miracle" has ended. Historians, philosophers or possibly poets will enlighten us. On the day of awakening, the words of Goethe will describe each one of us: "And here poor fool, with all my lore/I stand no wiser than before."

In the meantime, the clouds of parallels between previous sharp corrections and smashes are gathering. Here are some of the frightful hors d'oeuvres that usually herald the feast. A 10 percent unemployment rate in most of the Western world has become a fact of life. Six million unemployed out of a population of 65 million enthroned Hitler in Germany some 50 years ago. In

France today, the youth have taken to the streets, as always happens in Paris when the weather gets warmer. With unemployment running as high as 20 percent, there is little difficulty in assembling an array of troubleseekers in any capital. In the last 12 months, over 180 full or partial currency devaluations have occurred around the globe. It stands to reason that the intensity of monetary turbulence will grow as unemployment and deficits increase. Historically, a flurry of money printing started with tumult in the streets.

In the United States, the dream of a balanced budget by 1984 has been translated into a deficit now predicted by the Reagan administration to be in the $200 billion range for each of the next five years. This mammoth deficit exceeds the combined deficits of all U.S. governments for the 189 years between 1789 and 1978. With the tradition of overshooting deficit predictions by megaproportions, one can only assume, alas, that the $200 billion per year estimate will actually herald a much larger deficit.

The most acute problem, however, seems to be that the public at large has such great confidence in its leaders, not realizing that the leaders are even more confused than those who sent them to office. The 1983 Economic Summit Conference in Williamsburg is a good example.

The ghost of the 1982 Versailles Summit Conference was not exorcised in Williamsburg. The good tradition of yet another summit without substance was continued. The 1983 summit was, in reality, little more than a campaign rally for British Prime Minister Margaret Thatcher, who was seeking reelection. In view of the fact that all seven Western leaders had their feathers ruffled upon return from last year's summer vacation in the domain of Louis XIV, this year's emphasis was the official endorsement of inaction. In a world in which politicians have had it so easy in recent years, they definitely do not want to upset the apple cart. Behind closed doors some shouting occurred, particularly between France and the rest of the world, but talk about the return to fixed money exchanges *à la* Breton Woods and the good old times

156

of 1944 produced nothing. And a return to the gold standard will remain a dream as before.

Government paralysis in the face of the economic storm clouds now gathering means that dreams of endlessly rising stock market prices eventually must come to an end. In the meantime, those who do not want to put on their thinking caps or be bothered to analyze or study repetitive cycles and other ominous parallels to previous booms and busts should do extremely short-term trading. The bull, if not yet exhausted, is running out of steam.

So you can either take your profits and run, or be more aggressive and start selling short. Some stocks have moved up 200, 300 and 400 percent since 1983, but the show is almost over. Long-distance thinking with short-distance acting may produce today's only winners. As the old saying goes, "When you smell flowers, the casket cannot be far behind."

Good times breed bad times. The fast, loose encounters of the energy boom are over. From an historical angle, the parallels to 1929 are most revealing, if not shocking:

• An agricultural depression of falling farm prices and real estate collapses are much more severe than in 1929. Staple commodities such as sugar are selling at levels of a fraction of production price; below $.04 per pound of sugar versus $.11 of production cost.

• Huge pyramids of business debt are supported by a flimsy, almost nonexisting equity foundation. Speculators of 1985 are the same breed as of 1929, interested in fast trading rather than positioning themselves. Most traders today (as in 1929) maintain that a better than expected economy will keep on propelling up prices. However, margin debt is an ocean of red ink. The margin debt of the New York Stock Exchange members has soared during the recent explosion on Wall Street by $1 billion in three days to an all-time high of $24 billion. The ratio of margin to the New York Stock Exchange index now stands at an all-time high.

• A shaking banking system is supported "by never paying nonperforming loans." Even the FDIC has now some 900 American

157

banks on their problem list, a steep rise from 721 last year, which was a presidential election year. A survey shows that the list is much closer to 2,000 banks and thrift institutions, among them giants of no smaller caliber than Continental Illinois.

• The international debt is mounting in leaps and bounds, and a moratorium on all debts denominated in U.S. dollars should not be ruled out. This would entail a conservative write-off of over $1 trillion, in a time when servicing the U.S. domestic internal debt alone consumes nearly 80 percent of its collected tax dollars.

The expectation that inflation cures all mistakes is the last grasp of court economists and politicians. What is grossly overlooked is that historically a deep deflation must precede the inflationary fix. Establishment economic gurus will remain rose-colored by their own misunderstanding until the new reality of the mismanaged Reagan era finally emerges.

A further misunderstanding with regard to the immediate future of precious metals underlines the present reality. In a deflationary cycle, hard cash and not gold is king. The last three years were dispelling, at least for a short while, the popular belief that high levels of debt must breed hyperinflation and therefore propel gold to levels never seen before. While this is quite possible for 1987 and beyond, it is unlikely to take place before. The strongest support to this theory emanates from the correlation between the prices of oil and gold, which over the years were inextricably linked.

One barrel of crude oil equals 2.6 grams of gold; therefore, crude oil at $25 U.S. equals $210 per ounce of gold. If oil drops, as some industry analysts are predicting, to $12, gold may decline to the unbelievable level of $100. If this happens, the gold/silver ratio may widen to 1:60 from April 1985 levels of 1:49.

It should not be overlooked that gold and oil, on the eve of a possible deflation, are two minerals that are still selling at profit way above their production costs. The traditional oil- and gold-producing countries, the U.S.S.R. and South Africa, can produce gold at $80 per ounce. Russia, having both along with the Middle

Eastern producers, can extract oil for as low as $3 per barrel. The fact that OPEC at the moment is running a surplus of 1 million barrels a day, with cash prices at Rotterdam quoted as low as $24 per barrel, coupled with the fact that the lingering Iran/Iraq war and threatened blockage of Hormuz did not produce a sharp rise in the price of oil confirms that we are heading for lower oil prices, behind which gold will not be a laggard.

Do not confuse short-term potential developments with the overall picture. A lower short-term price for gold and silver can be exploited by those who wish to purchase additional quantities. Insurance should be liquidated only when insurance is not needed. If you are still in your earning years, engage in an afford-able cost-averaging program and forget the coins you put away. Just pray that you will not have to call on your gold too soon.

In the reality of 1984 and early 1985, when real interest pro-duced yields of 3 percent to 4 percent in first-class financial instruments, the nagging question remains: why did we not witness an overwhelming demand for U.S. government debt in-struments? The answer is quite simple. The market, being a dis-counting animal, provided well in advance and catered to accom-modate all the good news of the boom that did not materialize. Students of history may be identifying the last few years as one of the largest bull traps in history, when the public at large kept on ignoring the flashing signs of an imminent deflation.

This year and next should demonstrate and bear witness to a closing of the disparity between false perception and make-believe expectations which marked the beginning of the Reagan era. Ronald Reagan may well rue his reelection, because a second Hoover in American history is in the making.

16
STRATEGIC METALS

*"Grace is given of God, but knowledge
is bought in the marketplace."*
—ARTHUR HUGH CLOUGH

Metals have always been in demand for both military and civilian purposes. Metals have been labeled "strategic" if a shortage in them could greatly endanger a country's industrial or military potential and retard economic development. Recently, investors have been bombarded with literature promising huge profits from investing in strategic metals. The entrepreneurs maintain that anyone who now moves into that field will enjoy the same advantages as someone who bought gold at $35 an ounce.

The approach of most of the sales pitches is that an East-West resource confrontation is about to start, that the Russian invasion of Afghanistan, Soviet involvement in Nicaragua and the Middle East conflicts have renewed the cold war. The argument continues: since most of the strategic metals come from central and southern Africa, where independent states are now greatly influenced by Cuban and Russian forces, the United States and the West could be brought to their knees by a metal OPEC, formed by the suppliers of these metals. The sales talk stresses that you are bound to make money on your investment in strategic metals not because you are so bright, but because your Western government is so stupid not to have accumulated such materials in time.

Much of this is true. The reliance of the Western world on products such as nickel and chrome is so severe that the lack of chrome, for instance, could set Western civilization back by several decades. During 1980 the United States imported 91 percent of its chromium needs, while the remaining 9 percent came from recycled scrap. A few key minerals are the metallurgical Achilles' heel of the West. The United States should not be experiencing today the serious problem of being self-sufficient in only 5 out of 27 minerals considered essential to Western civilization. (The Russians are self-sufficient in 21 out of the 27.) Furthermore, the Russians are dependent on outside sources for no more than 50 percent of any of the 6 missing metals.

Nevertheless, investment literature touting strategic minerals is a prime example of negative salesmanship. This approach bets that a major world military crisis will soon arise and that somehow a few investors will escape the flames. Not only is this logic doubtful, it ignores the likelihood that in such a situation many nonstrategic minerals will be just as valuable.

When you accumulate gold or silver, you insure yourself against the ultimate collapse of the monetary system that has been deteriorating rapidly. You hope and believe that there is light at the end of the tunnel and that eventually, once order is restored, you will be able to spend your fortune. Before you are dragged into strategic metals, however, ask yourself whether there will be a world in which to spend your profits. Rest assured that if you and the world both survive, on the day cobalt sells for $100 per pound, platinum and palladium too will offer handsome rewards for those who own them.

Metals are usually segregated into three categories:

Precious Metals:	Gold	Platinum	Rhodium	
	Silver	Palladium		
Base Metals:	Aluminum	Lead	Tin	
	Copper	Nickel	Zinc	
Strategic Metals:	Antimony	Columbium	Manganese	Silicon
	Beryllium	Gallium	Mercury	Tantalum
	Bismuth	Germanium	Molybdenum	Tellurium

Cadmium	Indium	Osmium	Titanium
Cerium	Iridium	Rhenium	Tungsten
Chromium	Lithium	Ruthenium	Vanadium
Cobalt	Magnesium	Selenium	Zirconium

Of these metals, gold and silver serve as both money and commodities; all the others are commodities.

The following list shows how four major types of ore, which are representative of most of the others, are distributed geographically.

Platinum	*Manganese*	*Cobalt*	*Chromium*
93% South Africa	37% South Africa	56% Zaire	48% South Africa
5% Others	18% Others	18% Zambia	16% Soviet Union
2% Soviet Union	10% Brazil	6% Finland	10% Philippines
	8% Australia	4% Canada	8% Turkey
	7% Gabon	2% Botswana	8% Albania
	20% Processing	& S. Africa	8% Brazil
	only: pri-	14% Processing	2% Others
	marily France,	only: pri-	
	Norway	marily U.K.,	
		Norway	

Do not even attempt to enter the strategic metal market unless you have a portfolio of $1 to $2 million and wish to gamble $100,000. You would be foolish to risk more than 10 percent of your portfolio, and $100,000 is the minimum amount necessary to take a substantial position in any of the minerals. As the following chart shows, your initial investment *has* to be substantial.

Mineral	*Symbol*	*Contract Size*	*Grade*
Aluminum	Al	25 t	LME Spec.
Antimony	Sb	5 t	99.6% Regulus
Bismuth	Bi	1–5 t	99.99% Ingot
Cadmium	Cd	5 t	99.95% Ingot or Stick
Cerium	Ce	1,000 kg	99% Metal
Chromium	Cr	5–10 t	99% Lump
Cobalt	Co	1–5 t	Producer branded Cathode or Granule
Germanium	Ge	100 kg	Refined

162

Mineral	Symbol	Contract Size	Grade
Gold	Au	100 Troy oz	Fine Gold
Indium	In	500 oz	99.99% Ingot
Iridium	Ir	100 Troy oz	Sponge/Powder
Lead	Pb	25 t	LME Spec.
Lithium	Li	0.5 t	99.9% Ingot
Magnesium	Mg	10 t	Dow Peglock Grade I
Manganese	Mn	10 t	99.95% Electrolytic
Mercury	Hg	Flask × 20	99.99%
Molybdenum	Mo	10 t	Molybdenite Concentrate
Nickel	Ni	6 t	LME Spec. Metal
Osmium	Os	100 Troy oz	Fine Metal
Palladium	Pd	100 Troy oz	Fine Metal
Platinum	Pt	100 Troy oz	Fine Metal
Rhodium	Rh	50 Troy oz	Fine
Selenium	Se	10 × 100 lb Pots	99.5% or 99.8% Powder
Silicon	Si	10 t	98.5% Metal
Silver	Ag	10,000 Troy oz	Fine Silver LME Contract
Silver	Ag	1,000 oz	London Bullion
Tantalum	Ta	1,000 lb	99.9% Pins
Tellurium	Te	1,000 kg	99.5% Powder
Tin	Sn	5 t	LME Spec.
Titanium	Ti	5 t	99.6% Sponge
Tungsten	W	1 t	99.5% Powder
Vanadium	V	5 t	98% V_2O_5
Zinc	Zn	25 t	LME Spec.

t: tonne (2,205 lb)
lb: pound (2,205 lb: 1 t)

kg: kilogram (1,000 kg: 1 t)
LME: London Metal Exchange

In addition to the large amount of money you must be willing to invest, you may have to sit out such an investment for three years and lose 12 percent interest per annum. That is, your initial $100,000 must be worth at least $140,000 after 36 months just to make up for lost interest. Moreover, you must take into account brokerage fees of at least 2 percent on buy or sell, approximately $1.90 per week per ton storage, over 2 percent for administration and insurance per annum, and duties, which vary from country to country.

Strategic metals are commodities that have no international exchanges. They are in the hands of traders and brokers, and their buying and selling depends on the scruples of the brokers. Great opportunities for fraud abound in trading strategic minerals, particularly when a lower grade than was paid for is delivered to the merchant. The biggest problem with these metals is not how to get into the market, but how to get out. From the outset of the transaction, you are in the hands of the same entrepreneur and his merchant (who assembled your portfolio). You have to buy and sell at their price.

You will never see your strategic metals. All you will have is a piece of paper, a warrant, issued by a merchant stating that he has purchased the metals. Even a skeptic will not likely travel to London or Rotterdam to satisfy himself that the metals are indeed stored with the broker. Yet he may be sitting on a piece of paper issued by a mine owner in Zaire, Zambia or Zimbabwe. You may do better in Monte Carlo or Las Vegas; at least you would enjoy yourself while losing your money.

Investments in strategic metals have several more drawbacks. Most of these metals are and will remain the "spices" in "metal salads." Without the steel and iron deposits of Europe and North America, they are useless. Many of the metals are radioactive and/or carcinogenic. Other metals have to be warehoused in dehumidified or cooled facilities. Toxic fumes are a problem in the handling and storing of cadmium; oxidation is a problem with many others.

During the First World War, rubber was successfully replaced by plastics. A similar substitution could well happen to some strategic metals. Then you will have only unsound investments in extremely unsound hands.

Make sure that you purchase metals that have a potential market demand. If you are banking on an increase in the production of war materials, cobalt, titanium and germanium will probably be the most rewarding investments. All three are essential to the production of missiles, submarines and nuclear reactors, and so far no substitutes have been developed. According to the United

States Bureau of Mines, the price of cobalt went from $4 per pound in 1975 to $25 per pound in 1980; titanium went from $2.70 per pound to $7 per pound; and germanium went from $290 per kilogram (2.2 lb) to $750 per kilogram.

Cobalt, extracted from copper and nickel ores, is an essential additive in the production of steel, glass, high-temperature alloys and permanent magnets. In 1980 the United States imported 98 percent of its cobalt needs from the copper belt of Zambia and Zaire, a highly unstable political region. During the post-invasion period in 1979, a concentrated effort was made to airlift cobalt out of Zaire; but the entrepreneurs caused the price of cobalt, which had quadrupled during the abortive invasion, to drop to $23 per pound.

The addition of titanium to iron produces a much heavier-gauged stainless steel. This has enabled the Russians to develop a series of deep-water attack submarines. In the past the Soviet Union supplied approximately 50 percent of the world's titanium, but it has slowly withdrawn it from the market.

Germanium, a corrosion-resisting metal, is essential to the building of nuclear reactors. It is also essential in some products of the electronics industry. Most of the world's supply comes from South-west Africa (Namibia) and Zaire. Once Namibia achieves independence from South Africa, the 1980 price of $750 per kilogram may go much higher. However, the germanium market is rather thin. During late 1980 it was rumored that $12 million could corner the market. This makes germanium most vulnerable to a Hunt recipe.

The label "strategic" was coined on the premise that the Soviets may have the ability to cause the starvation of modern industry in the West by withholding or upsetting the flow of metals to the marketplace. How effective such an action would be remains to be seen. Even if such a sinister plot to deprive us of certain metals exists, germanium in the ground in Zaire or Zambia will not fill the bellies of their famine-stricken population; these countries will still need food from the West in exchange for their metals.

During periods of political distortion, the Western world may face great difficulties in obtaining certain metals. However, I doubt that by hoarding even several tons of cobalt, you will be able to enjoy a financial coup by selling it to your government for patriotic reasons or to a foreign power for sheer monetary rewards. If the world survives the economic calamity presently looming over it, industry may swiftly move from reverse to high forward gear. Platinum and palladium will become sought after as essential components of the peacetime revival of dormant industry. In many instances two ounces of palladium replace one ounce of platinum. The newly discovered "strategic" metals, however, may well move back into the oblivion they have occupied during past centuries.

Strategic metals can be profitable for those who make a living from them: mine owners, refiners, shippers, insurers, brokers and agents who wish to sell them. All these people make a profit by adopting a positive attitude—by mining, shipping and selling the metals; you are the only one who tries to make a profit by sitting on them. Only if the world goes up in flames, which may consume you, do you stand a chance of making a profit. The odds and the costs of acquiring strategic metals give you the wrong end of the stick.

I cannot close this chapter without mentioning a crucial warning to the individual trying to stock-pile strategic metals for the purpose of enriching himself on the eve of armageddon. Has it ever occurred to you that at a time for a call for strategic minerals, your government will just confiscate it? You may be paid, if at all, a fair market value which will be determined by a very nervous bureaucrat in the defence department. However, before paying, he will surely appeal to your patriotic sentiments to donate it to the war effort.

17
DIAMONDS: HAS THE GLITTER GONE?

"The secret of happiness is to admire without desiring.
And that is not happiness."
—F. H. BRADLEY

Diamonds were formed millions of years ago, when layers of carbon were subjected to intense heat and pressure. More recently, an enterprising South African, jealous of De Beers' monopoly of the diamond market, entertained the idea of capitalizing on the free and plentiful electrical discharges available in the Transvaal, an area blessed with electrical storms. He placed lumps of coal on top of strategically selected, lightning-vulnerable spots, hoping— as did his investors—that a lightning bolt would crystallize his carbon and flash him instant riches. Alas, what took nature millions of years to accomplish could not be performed in a moment, and the coal remained coal.

Today only some 2 percent of the gems are considered to be of investment quality. Generally, these stones weigh one karat or more and have few, if any, flaws. These stones do not go into the jewelry industry but are purchased as inflation hedges and as an investment. Although investment diamonds are relatively scarce, "relative" is the key word. At present there is an ample supply in terms of market demand.

If you buy an investment diamond, it is essential that you buy only high-quality stones and never less than one karat. Visually, there is little difference between a .95 karat stone and a 1.1 karat stone, and you may appear to be getting a bargain if a .95 karat stone is offered for $8,000 to $10,000 less than a 1.1 karat one. Beware of diamond "bargains."

Make sure that you have expert advice when you purchase a stone, and that the stone is properly authenticated by at least one internationally recognized certificate. Many firms offer certificates of authenticity for their stones. Some offer an insurance policy from Lloyds of London to indemnify purchasers in the event of a grading error. These certificates do not, however, offer an unconditional buy back. Indeed, you should beware of any dealer who does offer a guaranteed buy back. If the market goes down, he will be flooded with his previously sold stones and will almost certainly be unable to honor his pledge.

For generations there has been a very strong underground economy in diamonds. Stones are smuggled every day, in polished or uncut forms, from the producing countries to the polishing centers of Antwerp, Tel Aviv, Bombay and Hong Kong, and from those centers back to jewelers and investors. Of course, most investors in diamonds do not like to pay the import duties imposed by European and North American governments. Accordingly, they prefer to buy and sell diamonds in countries where they do not have to pay any taxes. Switzerland, Belgium, Israel and India do not have any taxes on exported stones, and very strong support economies in diamonds and other precious stones have developed in these countries.

The world is full of stories of refugees who made good their escape by hiding a few stones on their persons. A diamond can be much more easily hidden than gold or silver. The sensitive metal detectors that may reveal gold and silver on your body are not able to detect gemstones. However, once you reach a port of safety, you may find a diamond far more difficult to dispose of than gold. Large stones are not divisible, and you may lose precious time turning the stones into a more liquid asset. Moreover, in times of economic contraction, gemstones are usually affected far more by a declining market than are gold and silver.

Diamonds are largely controlled economically by one large distributor, the De Beers organization, which distorts, delays and often withholds from the gem investor crucial information that would enable him to move out of the market in time to realize a profit. Some gem dealers have had to backtrack on their claims that diamonds are accepted "like cash" and can be exchanged for currency in virtually any country. Recently, the Federal Trade Commission in the United States has taken a hard line against unscrupulous gemstone dealers who have made empty claims such as "prices have skyrocketed and have not declined for 45 years," and so on.

Diamond prices do, indeed, go up during times of inflation, but so do the prices of old comic books, porcelain dolls and a thousand other collectors' delights. The rule is simple: when prices in general are on an upward trend, namely when inflation is on the rampage, most articles increase in terms of depleted, available cash. At such times there are many other articles that could prove a better investment or hedge against inflation or chaos.

The diamond market is not as large as the gold market, and dealers in investment diamonds must mark up their merchandise between 50 percent and 100 percent to cover their overhead and marketing costs. If you buy a diamond through a magazine ad, in response to a direct mail appeal or at an investment conference, you are paying not only for the stone but also for the seller's cost of finding you as a customer, and a commission to the salesman who sold you the stone.

The diamond market has performed poorly in the last four years. A drop in diamond prices corresponded almost identically to the 39 percent drop in the profits of De Beers Consolidated Mines during the first half of 1981. A mining venture in Australia originally sponsored by De Beers has been put on hold, as a result of the present glut. The behavior of diamonds in the marketplace has proved that in times of high interest rates and a stagnant world economy, diamond prices perform poorly and gems rapidly lose their luster.

The present slump in demand for diamonds has been further

aggravated by an apparent change in attitude regarding luxury items since the end of the Second World War. While big stones bought and sold among jet-setters like Elizabeth Taylor and the Pahlavi family still make the gossip columns, investors have abandoned large gems. For them, it makes no difference whether they make their money on pork bellies or gems and, in recent years, hogs have offered the greater investment rewards. It could well be that in the 1960s and 1970s, diamonds were priced out of the market, and an investment-grade gem of one-karat-plus became an impossible gift for engagement and eternity rings. Instead, artificial crystals and diamond chips replaced the traditional solitaire diamond, further debasing the price of gemstones and contributing to the glut already on hand.

The tough times have had a snowballing effect within the cutting and polishing industry, and shock waves of commercial failures have reverberated through the diamond industry worldwide. Part of this drastic drop can be attributed to the expectations of cutters. Many of them turned speculators and hoarded large quantities of polished stones during 1978 and 1979 in anticipation of high profits. They overlooked the basic premise of the diamond game, that until recently it was run by one dynasty.

I say "until recently" because cracks are forming. Cash-starved Zaire, one of the largest diamond-producing countries in the world, has broken away from the De Beers organization. Guinea, another producer of some 25,000 karats per annum, has made moves to follow Zaire. It is estimated that the 80 percent of the diamond market controlled by the Oppenheimer family of South Africa and its London organization is shrinking.

However, diamonds might still be a girl's best friend, particularly if she has rich admirers or is an investor with a highly diversified portfolio. The general consensus is that after a 60 percent decline in just two years, diamond prices may be stabilizing. A bullish effect may result from De Beers' 7 percent to 10 percent cuts in mine output to enable existing stock to move from merchants to consumers.

An abrupt turnaround, however, is unlikely, as the fundamentals never change. Diamonds are indivisible or, rather, when divided yield only a chip of the original price. Diamonds may be forever, but not their prices, particularly when you want to sell your family heirlooms in a rush. If you have not yet made investments in jewels, therefore, better prices might be in the offing; but the consumer plagued by conflicting advice will find higher priorities and easier areas in which to capitalize on his free dollars than in gemstones.

18
RARE STAMPS AND OTHER COLLECTIBLES

"Never buy what you do not want ..."
—THOMAS JEFFERSON

Have you ever thought of the many proud owners of collectibles who are stuck with items they cannot sell? Even galleries like Sotheby's will never promise to repurchase a certain work from you after a specific time; all they will tell you is that their turn-over in 1978 or 1984 was close to $150 million. You are on your own when it comes to finding a buyer.

Many owners of collectibles found to their surprise in the early 1980s that the prices of many items available in various galleries have been bid up to such high levels that bargains have vanished. Collectibles can still be a sound investment, but only if you have knowledgeable advice and if you can enjoy what you collect.

Philately—stamp collecting—has in recent years become more sophisticated. The figures regarding new issues and past issues are far more accurate than those for rare coins. Most philatelic associations in Europe and North America have competent experts who can identify, evaluate and authenticate your rare stamps. It is essential when a novice starts with rare stamps that his portfolio be properly evaluated.

The best years of appreciation for North American stamps are from 1840 to 1900. Although dealers maintain that the supply is finite, and that there are only so many stamps available, occasionally "new" old stamps make their appearance on the market. Many of them are forgeries, but on a few occasions people discover that they have been sitting on treasures beyond their most optimistic expectations.

Condition can represent the difference between a valueless stamp and one of great value. A sneeze, a wrong touch or even being stored at the wrong temperature for any length of time can destroy the value of a stamp. It is only a piece of paper, after all.

Stamp collections are rarely accepted as collateral for loans by banks, but there are specialized dealers who are prepared to extend a loan to you on the basis of your stamp collection, usually at higher than prevailing rates of interest. Rare stamps have the advantage of being easily transportable. Metal detectors at airports will never detect them. They are not subject to duty, and they can be used for the repatriation of capital from one country to another. However, if you have to buy your freedom, a border guard or boat captain will not appreciate a stamp. An ounce of gold, however, will still buy you the value of an ounce of gold.

I have, but only for very wealthy investors and only for a small portion of their total worth, recommended rare stamps in selected investment portfolios. The smaller investor is likely to do better elsewhere.

Rare books and first editions, as well as books signed by the author or illustrator, have appreciated greatly in recent years and often command very high prices. Some books issued by the Limited Edition Club in 1930 for $10 now sell for $2,000 and more. People in the publishing industry maintain that any book limited to 2,000 or fewer copies may eventually become a collector's item if the author gains sufficient recognition. Today's novice may become tomorrow's old master—or his book may just take up space on your bookshelf.

To be a successful collector of rare books you should have a flair for a particular author or period of literature. There is no sense in hoarding antique books without being knowledgeable about the subject or particular book or author. At the same time, it is necessary to be wary of forgeries: remember the so-called "Hitler Diaries."

The same advice applies to autographs. Years ago you could not find a purchaser for an autograph of Hitler, but since 1980, his autographs have risen sharply in price. Several years ago, an autograph of Martin Luther King was almost worthless, but today it commands about the same price as an autograph of Abraham Lincoln. (Remember, though, that autographs of Lincoln and Hitler are the two most forged autographs in history.)

If you collect paintings by old masters, you should have a flair for a particular artist or period of art. Reputable art galleries maintain some interesting data on current artists as well, and an investment in such an artist could prove extremely rewarding over the years. I do not advise you, however, to cover your walls with a type of painting which you do not like. If you like geometric abstractions, fine; but if you enjoy landscapes, buy a landscape.

From 1968 to 1979, Chinese ceramics outperformed all investments, including gold and diamonds. In the United States, Chinese ceramics have maintained an 18 percent per annum increase in value over the past 10 years. With such collections, you must combine investment skill with an outstanding taste for beautiful ceramics and antique glassware. The danger in such investments is that you have no divisibility whatsoever, as you have in precious metals, and they are quite difficult to move with you if you must leave your home country.

In Western countries with relatively stable democratic governments, antique furniture has turned out to be an excellent investment and inflation hedge. One thousand dollars' worth of Early American furniture purchased in 1960 rose close to 500 percent in 20 years. Functional antique furniture is one of the few investments that gain in value while you use them; part of its value comes from the fact that an antique serves a function as well as being an art object. As with any investment, you should buy only from a reputable dealer, on the advice of a reputable appraiser who will, for a fee, authenticate the item and advise you if it is realistically priced.

Do not expect to become rich overnight from the purchase of

174

some antique furniture. It is one of those very few items you can enjoy, use and expect to increase in value over the long run. Antique furniture is usually not stolen from homes, and insurance costs are only the basic total loss and fire policy, which is relatively inexpensive. In unstable regimes, however, antique furniture may well turn out to be a white elephant if you must suddenly pack up and leave your home.

Investing in furniture and other collectibles makes sense if you live in a relatively stable country and if you have a specialized area of interest or knowledge. You must also have the time and patience to look for a buyer when you want to realize a profit on your investment. And on occasion, you must be prepared to have invested only in your own enjoyment of certain items for which no buyer can be found.

19
REAL ESTATE

"The buyer needs a hundred eyes..."
—GEORGE HERBERT

There are several major categories of real estate. First, of course, is the house you live in, your home. You invest in it and furnish it to suit yourself and your family. After all, most people would like to make their lives as peaceful and enjoyable as possible within their financial means.

You may also own a second home. If you own a weekend home that you can reach after a short drive, and if you can afford to maintain it, you should keep it: in times of urban unrest, such rural retreats may become lifesavers. However, it is foolish to invest in that "last stretch of white sand" on a warm island with an unstable government. Although the brochure now boasts that the island is a tax haven, the government may change and you may never learn what happened to the finance minister who was running the show when you first went there, or to the banker to whom you entrusted your assets. One sunny day they may be shot, incarcerated or disappear with your money.

Many dream condominiums, bathed in the green of golf courses, sprinkled with tennis courts and overlooking the blue oceans, tend to be oversold. Owners feel compelled to visit two or three times a year to "enjoy" their property. Eventually they may take stock and say, "Hey, I have not yet seen the world. Why do I bury myself alive here every year?"

During times of instability, that additional summer home in Florida or on the Spanish, Italian or French Riviera becomes meaningless if travel becomes difficult. If you own a jet and have a pilot on retainer, you need not read this chapter; but for most people, who enjoy only an annual or semiannual holiday, I see no great sense in maintaining a home, a condominium or a chalet that is linked to you only through your willingness and ability to travel long distances, sometimes internationally, by air.

Unless you are a real estate investor planning to rent your summer place to tourists, you will usually find that you are on the losing side. Even if your condominium in Fort Lauderdale or the south of France now sells for double the price you paid for it five years ago, you will easily find that had you taken those $25, $30 or even $50,000 and invested them in any of the items on the broader base of my investment pyramid, you would have done much better than with the condominium. (And do not forget the risk of exposure to taxation authorities, who may ask how you could afford an additional home on your declared income.)

A distinction has to be made between housing for one's own use and housing for speculative or investment purposes. There is no risk-free investment, and the very same fear that propels us into investing in gold and silver also has inflated the prices of real estate. When investing for speculative purposes or to escape from currency debasement, you must appreciate that declines in price may be precipitated by a variety of conditions beyond those of supply and demand. You have to identify problems pertinent to local markets and difficulties related to the national and world markets. If you are a real estate bug, bear in mind that the location of your investment is the prime consideration.

Your number one enemy, if you are a landlord, may be rent control. You will be faced with rising taxes and other mandatory expenses. Rent control will make sure that your income is held down artificially. Inflation kills the mortgage market, and you may find yourself a victim of the very inflation that enticed you to venture into real estate. Once you address yourself to the problem

177

of inflation and measure the rises in real estate values in terms of gold, you will find that, with some dramatic exceptions, prices of most properties are shockingly low in terms of gold. You will find that a property that was on the market in 1974 for $500,000 (4,000 ounces of gold at the time) could be yours in 1983 for one-quarter of that amount of gold.

Real estate is surely an inflation hedge, but as with any good inflation hedge, it may well be subjected to sharp dips in price, like gold. If you believe that hyperinflation is inevitable, the $1,000 down payment on a $10,000 home will yield 1,000 percent profit when the property doubles in price. This is true, of course, but only if you continue to believe in minidollars and gauge your income in fiat money instead of gold or another tangible yardstick of purchasing power.

If you become an expert on escaping inflation, there may be room for you to join the ranks of the very few who have made a fortune in real estate. But you must be a master of your art, because only a very few make it in any specialized field during times of uncertainty and inflation.

Another form of real estate to consider is productive, working farmland. Farmland is low on my priority list, although conventional wisdom has it that even in times of great anxiety, the land will still be there and the farmers will still be growing food and raising livestock. This is not necessarily so: in times of recession or depression, the cost of production of many goods—grains, dairy products and meat products—can easily exceed the market price these farm products can command. During such times only two types of farms are economically viable: family farms with little or no long-term debt and corporate farms whose parent companies are prepared to endure losses for years, possibly as a tax shelter to reduce taxes on other income.

A distinction must be drawn between farmland that you cultivate, such as a family farm where you make your living, and investment farmland. Investment farmland is land that an urban professional or businessman purchases as an inflation hedge in

178

times of an unstable economy. Farmland has a much greater chance to hold real values and appreciate during times of instability than does urban land. As long as you are bidding on land against and along with farmers, the price will reflect the land's agricultural value. If many other professionals or corporations are in the race, the price of agricultural land will be well beyond its real value. Speculation in farmland close to urban areas, which may eventually be purchased for housing or shopping centers, is not recommended, as the current price usually fully reflects the likelihood of such development.

The greatest disadvantage of farmland, of course, is that you can never take it with you. Times of instability can bring an enormous redistribution of land and reshuffling of ownership. I saw coffee farms in Angola being traded for one-way air tickets out of the troubled country. Some of the owners had their roots in the land for close to 400 years; but when a Marxist government took over that hopeless country, the Portuguese farmers who were able to exchange their homesteads for an air ticket to Lisbon came out ahead of the game. Angola is still racked by civil war, and its agriculture is in a state of collapse.

We are on the threshold of a very significant change in the world social order. The Western world is about to give in to enormous pressures coming from Third World countries, where some 70 percent of the population of the world are eagerly looking to the West for a redistribution of land, wealth and resources. The urge of several billion people on our earth is for a piece of land and "room to live." The days when you could defend your land against invaders with your double-barreled shotgun are over. Ask landowners in Mozambique, Iran or Cuba. In the name of a revolution, lucky owners may have their land confiscated in a matter of hours; unlucky ones remain attached to their land, six feet under.

My warnings against real estate investment may seem odd, as real estate has been the largest single base on which fortunes have been built since the Great Depression 50 years ago. But we are living in a very different era. Certain Western countries are already experiencing zero population growth. As the average age of the population in the Western world increases, the need for additional housing will decline, contrary to the patter of real estate developers. The decline in housing needs will cause additional problems in related industries: fewer carpets, kitchen appliances, vacuum cleaners and television sets will be sold, not to mention less timber, cement and the transportation of these products.

In addition, real estate is a uniquely local market, and no two local markets are identical. Real estate values today are depressed in parts of the industrial northeast of the United States, especially the Great Lakes area of Michigan, Pennsylvania, Ohio and Indiana. An office building in Montreal can be had for a fraction of its value, building prices in Calgary or Vancouver have collapsed since the burst of the oil bubble. Homes, offices and factories in Nicaragua, Jamaica, Zaire or Uganda can be had for a song, especially if the owner is paid in foreign currency outside the country where the property is located.

Even assuming a stable or appreciating market, there are disadvantages to real estate as a long-term investment: maintenance, interest, insurance and management costs inevitably increase. And, of course, taxes, zoning restrictions, rent control and outright confiscation.

Moreover, real estate is rarely purchased for cash. If panic selling should hit real estate in general, the high leverage—up to 90 or 95 percent—generally associated with such investments will cause prices to fall even faster. (For some strange reason, a real estate investment with 5 or 10 percent down is considered a good investment, while a soybean futures contract bought with a similar down payment or margin is considered highly speculative. Just as a few days' limit down movement can wipe out a commodity position, an unexpected softening in real estate prices can destroy a slim equity position.)

The real estate market has only so much real value. If a major segment of that real value is concentrated in a small spot, that

180

small spot is likely to grow at a phenomenal speed, as happened during the great gold rush. We have to make sure not to anchor ourselves in a place that may turn into a ghost town. If we do, we will be stuck there, for the bottom line of real estate is that it cannot be moved.

20
INVESTMENT
NEWSLETTERS

"I never think of the future. It comes soon enough."
—ALBERT EINSTEIN

Various advisory services, stock market and hard-money news-letters have mushroomed all over the Western world in recent years. Unfortunately, many of these letters are a means to an end for their publishers and increase their profits before offering any tangible aid to their readership. Publishers have discovered an ever-increasing market to which they can peddle their views. Most, if not all, of the newsletters survive and, indeed, thrive on fear. The uneducated and unsuspecting reader is prey for the easy money industry and the gloom and doom newsletters. Unfortunately, a high-quality and objective newsletter has become a rarity; many readers do not know how to select useful, reliable guidance.

Most large stockbrokers and trust companies issue their own newsletters, which they send to their clients free of charge. You can learn a lot from these publications. Some of their editors are quite knowledgeable, but these companies send you their letters primarily to serve their own interests. They obviously want to sell you something.

Only a handful of these letters prove to be consistent with their advice and philosophy, and only a very few publishers refrain from touting stocks, land deals, gems, books or other interests. Most have gone into the business of selling and renting their mailing lists, and recommending stocks or other investments in which they have a vested interest. If they recommend the purchase of survival kits, the proceeds from sales earn them a commission. When the oil shortage became acute, one newsletter offered gasoline canisters and at the same time sold travel packages and retirement schemes—all on commission from the publisher.

One of the glamor boys, who brags about his high hourly consultation fees, is clearly on the payroll of the South African government to promote its interests among hard-money people. Still other publishers, once their subscription bases exceed 2,000 or so, forget their humble beginnings and begin to parrot the Establishment line in hopes of appearing on "Wall Street Week" or being quoted in the *Wall Street Journal*.

With some 2,000 newsletters floating around the United States alone, it becomes a game of follow-the-leader. If 12 or 24 of the better-known publishers become either bullish or bearish, after some time, even if they were wrong, you will find many other newsletters following their lead. Most of them lack the means to maintain an expensive information system, and their views are a combination of gut feeling and plagiarism. They have stripped the newsletter industry of its vitality and originality of thought, which is what subscribers look for in a restricted, expensive newsletter. Many newsletter writers have turned their publications into postmortems or thermometers when, in fact, their readership is looking for a barometer.

Worst of all are the publishers who play the role of prophet and crusader to promote a self-invented mania. One slickly produced letter, which purports to give financial advice, after inveighing mightily against the welfare state favored its readers with the following observations: "This is the story of SOCIALISM, COMMUNISM and the ANTICHRIST!!! It's easy to quit hunting and sit back while Big Brother feeds, houses and clothes you. We've become a FAT (literally overweight), LAZY (gross national product proves this), DEPENDENT (one out of four works for the government) society of 'give me what's mine' people. Everyone wants as much government freebies as they can get." Obviously, people must subscribe to these theories, because this newsletter has been available for several years now.

The best and most amusing part of many newsletters is the subscription campaign. That's when you receive all the data proving how they were always right and called the shots weeks and months in advance. This reminds me of the story about the marksman who proudly displayed all the "bull's eyes" he had shot in recent years. When asked about his tremendous success he responded, "I never miss. First I shoot, and then I draw a target around the hole."

Newsletter writers today have found that if there is any money in capitalizing on their research and studies it is in the future, predicting interest rates and the direction of stocks and metals. Marcus Tullius Cicero observed 100 years before Christ, "Let us not go over old ground; let us rather prepare for what is to come." Imagine what a ball Cicero would have had on Wall Street if he had been a newsletter editor.

Have you ever noticed how some newsletter writers predict a catastrophe two or three years down the road? The predicted catastrophe may be hyperinflation, a depression, a banking collapse or even a nuclear war, but it is always two or three years away. It is not six months to a year away, or four or five years away, but two or three years away.

There's a reason for this. If the guru predicts something in the near future—six months to a year—and it doesn't come true, his readers notice his mistake and may not renew their subscription. Four or five years away is too far to really focus on; but two or three years is just right. That's just enough time for the guru to sell you multiple-year subscriptions, tapes, special reports and so on. And if it looks like his prediction was wrong, well, he has enough time to change gears, start a new two- or three-year cycle and hope you've forgotten his old one.

Hard-money newsletters tend to be bullish on gold at the same time, and stock market letters tend to tout stocks in unison. When all is said and done, each newsletter writer must promote what he discusses. Hard-money letters and stock market letters would, in the final analysis, lose their subscribers if the public did not have buying interest in precious metals and stocks. Bears, when they are right, are traitors to their cause. When they are wrong, they are held up to ridicule.

Even bulls, however, can miss the extent of a sudden move. In June 1979, some 30 experts on gold were interviewed and asked about their projections for that year. Not one projected $400 plus. How many foresaw on December 21, 1979, when gold closed at $489, that on the opening of business in 1980, gold would rocket and that in 15 trading days (on January 21) it would reach $850? Of course, when gold surpassed $600 on January 3, and the public lined up in subzero temperatures to purchase silver for $50 an ounce, 3,000 experts mushroomed and confirmed that $1,000 for gold in 1980 had been on their charts of sunspots and eclipses for the past 10 years.

The plethora of explanations for the rise in the price of gold from under $300 to over $500 in 1982–83 ranged from the plausible to the ridiculous. One service discovered that the price hike could be attributed to the possible failure of the Third World countries and the ensuing banking crisis. The ink had hardly dried when a new chunk of wisdom emerged: "Gold goes up in price because a large coin vendor in Arizona went belly up."

The early 1980s not only set a new record for stock prices, they also boasted an explosion of predictions that were subordinate to intense hope. The study of the markets, which has always been abstract, was reinforced by an army of mystical interpreters. Today's soothsayers persist in saying that the universe must behave according to their figures and must conform to a jigsaw puzzle of charts and software that they peddle. Economic cycles predetermined by Kondratieff, Elliott and their disciples overshadowed, overpowered and even manipulated the news. In times of record high unemployment, many people become enchanted with and captivated by metaphysics and mysticism. Aladdin's lamps are big sellers; astro-economics becomes a booming trade.

Many people have turned to numerology and the occult to explain the "significance" of market movements. Here is the reason cited by a numerologist as to why gold would not go through $460 per ounce during 1982. His article, written in December 1981, explained that the number 460 consists of the two important figures of 4 and 6, which total 10. This theory, he claimed, is further supported by the "fact" that in terms of Swiss francs, gold had not then surpassed the 1,000 Swiss francs per ounce of gold level, which again is "based" on 10 × 100.

We can only wonder what set of numbers our necromancer would come up with if we had a repetition of 1979–80, when the price of gold shot up 75 percent in 14 (!) trading days. Those of us not so "skilled" in numerology would do better to consider this set of figures: $1 + 9 + 2 + 9 = 21$, and so does $1 + 9 + 8 + 3$.

I have yet to meet the financial guru who holds God by His beard and never misses an in or out of the market. Very simply, if he were that clever he would not have to tout subscriptions to his rag, and he would not need your $200 per year to contribute to his rent and grocery costs. A lot of advisors tell you what and when to buy, and many pundits advise you on what to get rid of and when; the unfortunate part is that usually it is not the same guru. In August 1982, how many stock market gurus saw a 500-point rise in the Dow-Jones in less than a year?

The industry must strive on; rents and fancy appearances in seminars have to be justified. One should not be surprised if his favorite newsletter, which started with a very solid philosophy of insurance in terms of financial survival, moved into touting and selling tax shelters in the Turks and Caicos Islands, beach fronts in the Bahamas, banks in the Netherlands Antilles and ranches in Costa Rica. Many newsletters advise people to sell the cornerstones of their financial well-being and replace them with worthless investments in the Caribbean. It will not surprise me if someday a few hundred suckers will subscribe to a newsletter selling

186

land on the moon; after all, they wouldn't want to miss the great lunar, or lunatic, real estate explosion. If you are a newsletter publisher, do not underestimate the gullibility of Americans, and you are bound to make a buck.

By all means, subscribe to newsletters; get important information and data that your local newspapers do not carry or hide on some obscure inner page. After all, a newsletter is only a digest of news that should be of interest to you. You are paying the editor for reading other publications, listening to the news and condensing it for you in the form of a newsletter. But *you* must decide whose advice to accept and value; make sure that you do not accept all that you read in your favorite newsletter as Holy Writ. It is meant to open your mind, provoke your thoughts and minimize mistakes when you make your bottom-line investments. It is your ingenuity and toil that made you the money you are about to invest, so you must guard it as only "Little Me" can do. After all, your publisher also is only a "Little Me," but in business for himself.

APPENDICES

ARE YOU REALLY MAKING A PROFIT?

By following the instructions given with Tables I and II shown on the next pages, you can determine the nominal return you need to make on your investments and their real return after taxation and inflation.

Table I (Page 194) shows the nominal dollar rates of return one must achieve to maintain the real purchasing power of assets under different taxation and inflation rates. Inflation rates are listed from 2½ percent to 200 percent across the top and bottom of the table; taxation rates from 0 percent to 90 percent are listed vertically at left and right.

For example, with a 20 percent inflation and a 40 percent tax rate, read down the 20 percent column and across the 40 percent row. The figure where they merge, 33.3 percent, is the nominal return you need to make to maintain purchasing power under these conditions.

Faced with a 40 percent inflation and a 20 percent tax rate, you need to make a higher nominal return: namely 50 percent.

Read Table II (Page 195) for calculating real returns of 10 percent after taxation and inflation.

Evaluating Your Position

To evaluate your position over any period you will need the following information:

- the total value of your assets (minus liabilities) at the two dates,
- total taxes paid, and
- the rate of inflation over that period (or the expected rate for setting future targets).

The total change in your net asset position, including income and capital profits (plus capital profits not actually taken) gives you the total nominal return on the value of your assets at the outset. (The return divided by the asset value and multiplied by 100 gives the percentage return.)

Taxes paid divided by your total nominal return and multiplied by 100 gives you the overall tax rate.

Having calculated thus far, you can determine how well you performed last year, and set your goals for the coming year.

Example: a U.S. resident has assets valued at $150,000 on December 31, 1983. During the year he received $3,500 income from these assets. His overall net asset position had increased to $172,000. He has a capital gain of $22,000 plus an income of $3,500, totaling $25,500. He achieved a 17 percent return on his assets. Because he had some money in Swiss francs and gold in Switzerland, his overall tax liability was now $4,900, or 19.2 percent.

Refer to Table III (page 196) and, taking U.S. inflation in 1984 at 6 percent, using the 5 percent column as an approximation to the inflation rate and 20 percent as close to the tax rate, we find he needed a 6¼ percent return to maintain his real purchasing power, so he did better. But he required a 19.4 percent return to make a real profit of 10 percent.

Suppose he assumes his overall tax rate for 1984 will remain the same, but for safety's sake anticipates inflation at 7½ percent.

His target for 1984 will be a minimum of 9.4 percent. This maintains his purchasing power intact. To make a 10 percent real profit, his return will have to increase to 22.8 percent, slightly more than in 1983.

Analyzing Individual Investments

Analyzing individual investments or business opportunities is the same: calculate the change in net asset position (both capital gains and income) and the taxes accruing from that particular investment.

You can now analyze your investment portfolio and determine which past investments maintained their purchasing power. Consider future investments on the basis of their performance after taxation and inflation.

Table 1: INVESTMENT RETURNS REQUIRED TO MAINTAIN CONSTANT PURCHASING POWER UNDER VARYING INFLATION AND TAXATION RATES

Taxation Rates								Inflation Rates									
	2.5%	5.0%	7.5%	10.0%	12.5%	15.0%	17.5%	20.0%	25.0%	30.0%	35.0%	40.0%	45.0%	50.0%	75.0%	100.0%	200.0%
0%	2.5%	5.0%	7.5%	10.0%	12.5%	15.0%	17.5%	20.0%	25.0%	30.0%	35.0%	40.0%	45.0%	50.0%	75.0%	100.0%	200.0%
10%	2.8%	5.6%	8.3%	11.1%	13.9%	16.7%	19.4%	22.2%	27.8%	33.3%	38.9%	44.4%	50.0%	55.6%	83.3%	111.1%	222.2%
20%	3.1%	6.3%	9.4%	12.5%	15.6%	18.8%	21.9%	25.0%	31.3%	37.5%	43.8%	50.0%	56.3%	62.5%	93.8%	120.0%	250.0%
30%	3.6%	7.1%	10.7%	14.3%	17.9%	21.4%	25.0%	28.6%	35.7%	42.9%	50.0%	57.1%	64.3%	71.4%	107.1%	142.9%	285.7%
40%	4.2%	8.3%	12.5%	16.7%	20.8%	25.0%	29.2%	33.3%	41.7%	50.0%	58.3%	66.7%	75.0%	83.3%	125.0%	166.7%	333.3%
50%	5.0%	10.0%	15.0%	20.0%	25.0%	30.0%	35.0%	40.0%	50.0%	60.0%	70.0%	80.0%	90.0%	100.0%	150.0%	200.0%	400.0%
60%	6.3%	12.5%	18.8%	25.0%	31.3%	37.5%	43.8%	50.0%	62.5%	75.0%	87.5%	100.0%	112.5%	125.0%	187.5%	250.0%	500.0%
70%	8.3%	16.7%	25.0%	33.3%	41.7%	50.0%	58.3%	66.7%	83.3%	100.0%	116.7%	133.3%	150.0%	166.7%	250.0%	333.3%	666.7%
80%	12.5%	25.0%	37.5%	50.0%	62.5%	75.0%	87.5%	100.0%	125.0%	150.0%	175.0%	200.0%	225.0%	250.0%	375.0%	500.0%	1000.0%
90%	25.0%	50.0%	75.0%	100.0%	125.0%	150.0%	175.0%	200.0%	250.0%	300.0%	350.0%	400.0%	450.0%	500.0%	750.0%	1000.0%	2000.0%
	2.5%	5.0%	7.5%	10.0%	12.5%	15.0%	17.5%	20.0%	25.0%	30.0%	35.0%	40.0%	45.0%	50.0%	75.0%	100.0%	200.0%

Taxation Rates

Inflation Rates

Table II: INVESTMENT RETURNS REQUIRED TO MAKE REAL 10% PROFIT UNDER VARYING INFLATION AND TAXATION RATES

Taxation Rates	Inflation Rates																
	2.5%	5.0%	7.5%	10.0%	12.5%	15.0%	17.5%	20.0%	25.0%	30.0%	35.0%	40.0%	45.0%	50.0%	75.0%	100.0%	200.0%
0%	12.8%	15.5%	18.3%	21.0%	23.8%	26.5%	29.3%	32.0%	37.5%	43.0%	48.5%	54.0%	59.5%	65.0%	92.5%	120.0%	230.0%
10%	14.2%	17.2%	20.3%	23.3%	26.4%	29.4%	32.5%	35.6%	41.7%	47.8%	53.9%	60.0%	66.1%	72.2%	102.8%	133.3%	255.6%
20%	15.9%	19.4%	22.8%	26.3%	29.7%	33.1%	36.6%	40.0%	46.9%	53.8%	60.6%	67.5%	74.4%	81.3%	115.6%	150.0%	287.6%
30%	18.2%	22.1%	26.1%	30.0%	33.9%	37.9%	41.9%	45.7%	53.6%	61.4%	69.3%	77.1%	85.0%	92.9%	132.1%	171.4%	328.6%
40%	21.3%	25.8%	30.4%	35.0%	39.6%	44.2%	48.8%	53.3%	62.5%	71.7%	80.8%	90.0%	99.2%	108.3%	154.0%	200.0%	383.3%
50%	25.5%	31.0%	36.5%	42.0%	47.5%	53.0%	58.5%	64.0%	75.0%	86.0%	97.0%	108.0%	119.0%	130.0%	185.0%	240.0%	460.0%
60%	31.9%	38.8%	45.6%	52.5%	59.4%	66.3%	73.1%	80.0%	93.8%	107.5%	121.3%	135.0%	148.8%	162.5%	231.3%	300.0%	575.0%
70%	42.5%	51.7%	60.8%	70.0%	79.2%	88.3%	97.5%	106.7%	125.0%	143.3%	161.7%	180.0%	198.0%	216.7%	308.3%	400.0%	746.7%
80%	63.8%	77.5%	91.3%	105.0%	118.8%	132.5%	146.3%	160.0%	187.5%	215.0%	242.5%	270.0%	297.5%	325.0%	462.5%	600.0%	1150.0%
90%	127.5%	155.5%	182.5%	210.0%	237.5%	265.0%	292.5%	320.0%	375.0%	430.0%	485.0%	540.0%	595.0%	650.0%	925.0%	1200.0%	2300.0%
	2.5%	5.0%	7.5%	10.0%	12.5%	15.0%	17.5%	20.0%	25.0%	30.0%	35.0%	40.0%	45.0%	50.0%	75.0%	100.0%	200.0%

Inflation Rates

Table III: Interest Rates and Inflation

Interest rates after taxes	Inflation rates																	
	3%	4%	5%	6%	7%	8%	9%	10%	11%	12%	13%	14%	15%	16%	17%	18%	19%	20%
3%	-0-	(-1)	(-2)	(-3)	(-4)	(-5)	(-6)	(-7)	(-8)	(-9)	(-10)	(-11)	(-12)	(-13)	(-14)	(-15)	(-16)	(-17)
3.5%	+0.5	(-0.5)	(-1.5)	(-2.5)	(-3.5)	(-4.5)	(-5.5)	(-6.5)	(-7.5)	(-8.5)	(-9.5)	(-10.5)	(-11.5)	(-12.5)	(-13.5)	(-14.5)	(-15.5)	(-16.5)
4%	+1	-0-	(-1)	(-2)	(-3)	(-4)	(-5)	(-6)	(-7)	(-8)	(-9)	(-10)	(-11)	(-12)	(-13)	(-14)	(-15)	(-16)
4.5%	+1.5	+.5	(-0.5)	(-1.5)	(-2.5)	(-3.5)	(-4.5)	(-5.5)	(-6.5)	(-7.5)	(-8.5)	(-9.5)	(-10.5)	(-11.5)	(-12.5)	(-13.5)	(-14.5)	(-15.5)
5%	+2	+1	-0-	(-1)	(-2)	(-3)	(-4)	(-5)	(-6)	(-7)	(-8)	(-9)	(-10)	(-11)	(-12)	(-13)	(-14)	(-15)
5.5%	+2.5	+1.5	+0.5	(-0.5)	(-1.5)	(-2.5)	(-3.5)	(-4.5)	(-5.5)	(-6.5)	(-7.5)	(-8.5)	(-9.5)	(-10.5)	(-11.5)	(-12.5)	(-13.5)	(-14.5)
6%	+3	+2	+1	-0-	(-1)	(-2)	(-3)	(-4)	(-5)	(-6)	(-7)	(-8)	(-9)	(-10)	(-11)	(-12)	(-13)	(-14)
6.5%	+3.5	+2.5	+1.5	+0.5	(-0.5)	(-1.5)	(-2.5)	(-3.5)	(-4.5)	(-5.5)	(-6.5)	(-7.5)	(-8.5)	(-9.5)	(-10.5)	(-11.5)	(-12.5)	(-13.5)
7%	+4	+3	+2	+1	-0-	(-1)	(-2)	(-3)	(-4)	(-5)	(-6)	(-7)	(-8)	(-9)	(-10)	(-11)	(-12)	(-13)
7.5%	+4.5	+3.5	+2.5	+1.5	+0.5	(-0.5)	(-1.5)	(-2.5)	(-3.5)	(-4.5)	(-5.5)	(-6.5)	(-7.5)	(-8.5)	(-9.5)	(-10.5)	(-11.5)	(-12.5)
8%	+5	+4	+3	+2	+1	-0-	(-1)	(-2)	(-3)	(-4)	(-5)	(-6)	(-7)	(-8)	(-9)	(-10)	(-11)	(-12)
8.5%	+5.5	+4.5	+3.5	+2.5	+1.5	+0.5	(-0.5)	(-1.5)	(-2.5)	(-3.5)	(-4.5)	(-5.5)	(-6.5)	(-7.5)	(-8.5)	(-9.5)	(-10.5)	(-11.5)
9%	+6	+5	+4	+3	+2	+1	-0-	(-1)	(-2)	(-3)	(-4)	(-5)	(-6)	(-7)	(-8)	(-9)	(-10)	(-11)
9.5%	+6.5	+5.5	+4.5	+3.5	+2.5	+1.5	+0.5	(-0.5)	(-1.5)	(-2.5)	(-3.5)	(-4.5)	(-5.5)	(-6.5)	(-7.5)	(-8.5)	(-9.5)	(-10.5)
10%	+7	+6	+5	+4	+3	+2	+1	-0-	(-1)	(-2)	(-3)	(-4)	(-5)	(-6)	(-7)	(-8)	(-9)	(-10)
10.5%	+7.5	+6.5	+5.5	+4.5	+3.5	+2.5	+1.5	+0.5	(-0.5)	(-1.5)	(-2.5)	(-3.5)	(-4.5)	(-5.5)	(-6.5)	(-7.5)	(-8.5)	(-9.5)
11%	+8	+7	+6	+5	+4	+3	+2	+1	-0-	(-1)	(-2)	(-3)	(-4)	(-5)	(-6)	(-7)	(-8)	(-9)
11.5%	+8.5	+7.5	+6.5	+5.5	+4.5	+3.5	+2.5	+1.5	+0.5	(-0.5)	(-1.5)	(-2.5)	(-3.5)	(-4.5)	(-5.5)	(-6.5)	(-7.5)	(-8.5)
12%	+9	+8	+7	+6	+5	+4	+3	+2	+1	-0-	(-1)	(-2)	(-3)	(-4)	(-5)	(-6)	(-7)	(-8)
12.5%	+9.5	+8.5	+7.5	+6.5	+5.5	+4.5	+3.5	+2.5	+1.5	+0.5	(-0.5)	(-1.5)	(-2.5)	(-3.5)	(-4.5)	(-5.5)	(-6.5)	(-7.5)
13%	+10	+9	+8	+7	+6	+5	+4	+3	+2	+1	-0-	(-1)	(-2)	(-3)	(-4)	(-5)	(-6)	(-7)
13.5%	+10.5	+9.5	+8.5	+7.5	+6.5	+5.5	+4.5	+3.5	+2.5	+1.5	+0.5	(-0.5)	(-1.5)	(-2.5)	(-3.5)	(-4.5)	(-5.5)	(-6.5)
14%	+11	+10	+9	+8	+7	+6	+5	+4	+3	+2	+1	-0-	(-1)	(-2)	(-3)	(-4)	(-5)	(-6)

KEY TO THE FUTURE: GUNN SQUARES

Every method used to predict the price of precious metals or other commodities has both its disciples and its opponents. Cycles of the full moon have been related to the prices of grain. Kondratieff and Elliott waves have greatly influenced futurists who, more often than not, ended up with egg on their faces for calling the wrong shots—like the one who announced from the podium that "my pricing was right—my timing was wrong." He was out by "only" 16 months.

Over the centuries, chartists have tried to find the Rock of Wisdom. They are still looking for it, along with alchemists craving to transform lead into gold. Here is some food for thought: no credit will be claimed if you happen to find the secrets into the future by tracing the price of gold on a Gunn Square.

Gunn Squares were developed by W. D. Gunn, a mathematician who excelled during the Roaring Twenties right through the Great Depression. He developed many trading strategies, squares of mathematical sequences being one of them. By moving from one number to another in increments of one unit, a sequence of numbers develops which, if read diagonally as highlighted in the following chart, reveals certain key levels.

Forty dollars matches the official price of $42.50 employed by most central banks since Nixon's reevaluation 12 years ago. The

$200 tag at the end of 1974 was then the highest price ever for gold. From $200 we witnessed a drop to $100 before gold again started its rise toward $1,000 per ounce. The magical $1,000 is in the seventh cycle, drawn diagonally from the starting point of $20.

After reaching $850 about three years ago, the price of gold declines and the left hand diagonal, according to the Gunn Square, corresponds well to the highs, and thereafter to the drops in price to $740, $620 and $480.

What is the next move? If it is only guesswork, then your forecast is probably as good as that of anyone who charges you several hundred dollars to subscribe to his predictions. By now we all know that panics are the outcome of surprises.

Table IV: GÚNN SQUARES

1220	1225	1230	1235	1240	1245	1250	1255	1260	1265	1270	1275	1280	1285	1290	1295
1215	930	935	940	945	950	955	960	965	970	975	980	985	990	995	1000
1210	925	680	685	690	695	700	705	710	715	720	725	730	735	740	1005
1205	920	675	470	475	480	485	490	495	500	505	510	515	520	745	1010
1200	915	670	485	300	305	310	315	320	325	330	335	340	525	750	1015
1195	910	665	460	295	170	175	180	185	190	195	200	345	530	755	1020
1190	905	660	455	290	165	80	85	90	95	100	205	350	535	760	1025
1185	900	655	450	285	160	75	30	35	40	105	210	355	540	765	1030
1180	895	650	445	280	155	70	25	20	45	110	215	360	545	770	1035
1175	890	645	440	275	150	65	60	55	50	115	220	365	550	775	1040
1170	885	640	435	270	145	140	135	130	125	120	225	370	555	780	1045
1165	880	635	430	265	260	255	250	245	240	235	230	375	560	785	1050
1160	875	630	425	420	415	410	405	400	395	390	385	380	565	790	1055
1155	870	625	620	615	610	605	600	595	590	585	580	575	570	795	1060
1150	865	860	855	850	845	840	835	830	825	820	815	810	805	800	1065
1145	1140	1135	1130	1125	1120	1115	1110	1105	1100	1095	1090	1085	1080	1075	1070

MORE ABOUT GOLD

The Weight of Gold

1 Troy ounce	31.1033 grams
1 Troy ounce	480 grains
1 Troy ounce	20 pennyweight (DWT)
12 Troy ounces	1 pound Troy
14 Troy ounces	1 pound avoirdupois
0.9114 Troy ounce	1 ounce avoirdupois
32.15 Troy ounce	1 kilogram
1 gram	5.3 karats (Roman)
1 gram	15.432 grains
1 gram	0.643 pennyweight (DWT)
1.5552 grams	1 pennyweight (DWT)
1,000 grams	1 kilogram
28.3495 grams	1 ounce avoirdupois
24 grains	1 pennyweight (DWT)
5,760 grains	1 pound Troy
15,432 grains	1 kilogram
437.5 grains	1 ounce avoirdupois
7,000 grains	1 pound avoirdupois
1 grain	0.0648 grams
240 pennyweight (DWT)	1 pound Troy
643.01 pennyweight (DWT)	1 kilogram
18.2291 pennyweight (DWT)	1 ounce avoirdupois
291.666 pennyweight (DWT)	1 pound avoirdupois
1 kilogram	2.68 pounds Troy
1 kilogram	35.2740 ounces avoirdupois
1 kilogram	2.2046 pounds avoirdupois

Metric versus Troy

The Troy System is currently used for weighing precious metals in Canada and in the United States. It is divided as follows:

1, Troy pound	12 Troy ounces
1 Troy ounce	20 pennyweights
1 pennyweight	24 grains

The Troy System is now being replaced in the United States and Canada with the Metric System. The Metric System is currently in use in all of Europe, Latin America and most other countries in the world. The weight of precious metals will then be expressed as follows:

1 tonne	1,000 kilos
1 kilo	1,000 grams
1 gram	1,000 milligrams

Fineness (Fine Gold)

Pure gold is 24 karats. The fineness is expressed in thousand parts of an alloy. Pure gold is 1.000 or 24 karats. Seven hundred and fifty parts of gold contained in 1,000 parts of alloy (.750) is known as 18 karats. The relationship of fineness to karats is proportional.

Fineness (or Purity) of Gold

24	Karats – 1,000	Fine		20	Karats – 833.3	Fine
23	Karats – 958.3	Fine		18	Karats – 750	Fine
22	Karats – 916.6	Fine		16	Karats – 666.7	Fine
21.6	Karats – 900.0	Fine		14	Karats – 583.3	Fine
21	Karats – 875.0	Fine		1	Karat – 41.7	Fine

World Gold Production

Reports on the daily volume of gold traded are somewhat misleading. On the New York Comex alone, daily trading may be as high as 150 tons. This, of course, is made up mainly by specu-

Table V: GOLD MINE PRODUCTION IN THE NON-COMMUNIST WORLD

(Metric Tons)	1973	1974	1975	1976	1977	1978	1979	1980	1981	1982	1983
South Africa	855.2	758.6	713.4	713.4	699.9	706.4	705.4	675.1	657.6	664.3	679.7
Canada	60.0	52.2	51.4	52.4	54.0	54.0	51.1	50.6	52.0	64.7	70.7
United States	36.2	35.1	32.4	32.2	32.0	31.1	29.8	30.2	42.9	45.0	50.4
Other Africa:											
Zimbabwe	10.5	10.4	11.0	12.0	12.5	12.4	12.0	11.4	11.6	13.4	14.1
Ghana	25.0	19.1	16.3	16.6	16.9	14.2	11.5	10.8	13.0	13.0	11.8
Zaire	2.5	4.4	3.6	4.0	3.0	1.0	2.3	3.0	3.2	4.2	6.0
Other	1.7	1.5	1.5	1.5	1.5	2.0	2.5	8.0	12.0	15.0	15.0
Total Other Africa	39.7	35.4	32.4	34.1	33.9	29.6	28.3	33.2	39.8	45.6	46.9
Latin America:											
Brazil	11.0	13.8	12.5	13.6	15.9	22.0	25.0	35.0	35.0	34.8	51.0
Chile	3.2	3.7	4.1	3.0	3.0	3.3	4.3	6.5	12.2	18.9	19.8
Colombia	6.7	8.2	10.8	10.3	9.2	9.0	10.0	17.0	17.7	15.9	17.9
Dominican Republic	—	—	3.0	12.7	10.7	10.8	11.0	11.5	12.8	11.8	10.8
Peru	2.6	2.7	2.9	3.0	3.4	3.9	4.7	5.0	7.2	6.9	9.9
Mexico	4.2	3.9	4.7	5.4	6.7	6.2	5.5	5.9	5.0	5.2	6.3
Nicaragua	2.4	2.3	2.2	1.9	2.0	2.0	1.1	1.9	1.9	1.6	1.7
Other	4.7	2.2	1.9	5.0	5.0	5.2	3.7	5.9	8.1	10.0	16.5
Total Latin America	34.8	36.8	42.1	54.9	55.9	62.4	65.3	88.7	99.9	105.1	133.9
India	3.3	3.2	3.0	3.3	2.9	2.8	2.7	2.6	2.6	2.2	2.2

Far East:											
Philippines	13.1	17.3	16.1	16.3	19.4	20.2	19.1	22.0	24.9	31.0	33.3
Japan	6.2	4.5	4.7	4.6	4.8	4.9	4.4	4.2	3.5	3.8	3.6
Other	2.7	2.7	2.7	3.0	3.0	3.5	4.0	4.5	4.6	5.2	5.3
Total Far East	27.0	24.5	23.5	23.9	27.2	28.6	27.5	30.7	33.0	40.0	42.2
Europe	14.3	11.6	11.0	11.4	13.2	12.5	10.0	8.6	8.5	10.6	10.00
Oceania:											
Australia	17.2	16.2	16.3	15.4	19.2	20.1	18.6	17.0	18.4	27.0	32.2
Papua/New Guinea	20.3	20.5	17.9	20.5	22.3	23.4	19.7	14.3	17.2	17.8	18.4
Other	2.8	2.2	2.2	2.3	1.8	1.1	1.0	1.0	1.1	1.2	1.6
Total Oceania	40.3	38.9	36.4	38.2	43.3	44.6	39.3	32.3	36.7	46.0	52.2
Total	1110.8	996.3	945.6	963.8	962.3	972.0	959.4	952.0	973.0	1023.5	1088.2

lators and risk takers who are betting on the direction of the market.

It is estimated that the average daily volume in the London bullion market is seven tons. In the last few years, the "EFP" market developed, and accounts for ten to fifteen tons overnight. "EFP" —exchange for physical—is a term used by professional traders for trades done outside exchange hours in the cash market and then transferred to the exchange books by clearing houses.

New production of gold is only about 1,400 tons per annum: approximately 1,000 tons produced by the Western world and 400 tons produced by the Communist bloc. The following figures compiled from the Gold Institute offer an overview of where the 1,000 tons of the Western world comes from.

It should be noted that in late 1984, Australia, Papua and Canada announced new gold finds, which may raise Canada's gold output to 85 tons per annum, Australia's to 40 tons and Papua's to 24 tons.

BANKING

The greatest problem plaguing the West that will remain with us for the foreseeable future is a confidence crisis. Banks fail when clients' confidence erodes. In 1984 more than 80 banks in the United States failed—the largest number since the Great Depression. If the years 1983, 1984 and 1985 set a pattern, then 1985–86 through 1990 should see more and more U.S. and Western world banks crumbling under the weight of nonconfidence. Remember, banks are only as good as those who make them: the depositors on one side, who deposit their hard-earned money as long as they have confidence in the institution, and the bankers who are entrusted with such funds and are expected to repay principal and interest. It is important to note that the U.S. banks that failed were, with the exception of Continental Illinois, relatively small banks that had nothing to do with Brazil and Zaire. The erosion is from within, which renders the crisis far more acute.

Until a few years ago, bank managers could operate on the 3:6:3 formula: pay for money at 3 percent, lend it out at 6 percent and at 3:00 P.M. tee off at the golf club. Those cosy days are gone, at least for the time being. Banks are and will feel the reality that the 1980s turn out to be a buyer's and not a seller's market. It has already happened in Europe and is beginning in the United States. Canada always lags three to five years behind the Americans.

Fifty Weakest Banks (With Assets Over $25 Million)

	Total Assets $ Mil.	Total Equity $ Mil.	Equity as % of Total Assets	Total Loans $ Mil.	Loan Loss Reserves as % of Total Loans	Loans 90 Days Past Due $ Mil.	% Equity	Non-Performing Loans $ Mil.	Renegotiated Loans $ Mil.	Brokered Deposits % Deposits
* 1. First Nat'l Bank of Midland, TX	$1409.6	$0.8	0.1%	$1101.4	7.7%	$110.7	765.7%	$307.1	0.0	12.2%
2. Nat'l Republic Bank of Chicago, IL	34.2	0.1	0.2	16.8	6.2	1.5	873.6	2.2	0.2	0.0
3. Decatur County Nat'l Bank of Oberlin, KS	25.1	0.1	0.2	19.5	3.4	0.8	486.8	0.0	0.4	0.0
4. Bank of Commerce, Morristown, TN	88.8	0.3	0.3	58.0	0.0	4.6	545.0	4.5	0.4	17.9
5. Citizens State Bank of NJ, Lacey Township, NJ	89.4	0.6	0.7	61.6	1.2	0.6	97.3	4.1	0.2	2.4
6. First Suburban National Bank, Maywood, IL	33.8	0.3	0.8	16.6	5.9	0.2	59.4	2.0	0.0	0.0
7. Bank of the Commonwealth, Detroit, MI	832.5	8.1	1.0	514.6	1.6	3.8	46.8	16.2	17.9	0.0
8. Union County Bank, Maynardsville, TN	52.6	0.8	1.5	26.5	1.1	4.8	624.9	4.6	0.0	22.7
* 9. Security Nat'l Bank of Lubbock, TX	64.2	0.9	1.3	49.2	4.8	1.4	161.4	3.7	0.0	5.7
*10. Farmers Bank & Trust Company, Winchester, TN	48.6	0.7	1.4	33.2	0.4	0.2	27.0	2.1	0.0	0.0
11. First State Bank of Idabel, OK	36.1	0.6	1.8	25.4	2.1	1.3	202.4	2.1	0.0	0.0

12. Fidelity Bank of Denver, CO	72.1	1.6	2.3	47.5	1.0	1.7	105.3	1.3	0.0	0.0
13. Seattle-First National Bank, Seattle, WA	8274.5	228.7	2.8	6300.1	4.6	50.1	21.9	725.2	74.1	2.8
14. First Pacific Bank, Beverly Hills, CA	80.9	2.3	2.9	54.7	1.0	1.8	75.8	1.6	1.1	10.6
15. Centennial Bank, Springfield, OR	66.7	1.5	2.2	41.5	4.2	0.6	38.6	2.3	0.3	0.0
16. First Southern Bank, Mount Juliet, TN	27.7	0.7	2.4	17.8	0.4	1.1	171.6	1.8	0.0	0.0
*17. Nat'l Bank and Trust Co. of Traverse City, MI	120.3	3.3	2.7	67.2	1.9	2.7	83.4	4.5	3.4	0.0
18. Keeseville National Bank, Keeseville, NY	43.0	1.0	2.4	24.2	3.1	0.4	42.5	1.1	1.8	0.0
*19. Union Trust Company, San Juan, PR	30.6	0.9	3.0	18.5	1.5	3.3	416.3	3.3	0.0	0.0
20. Lawrence County Bank, Lawrenceburg, TN	26.2	0.6	2.5	15.7	2.0	0.3	53.1	1.7	0.2	0.0
21. Wheeling Trust & Savings Bank, Wheeling, IL	110.1	3.1	2.8	61.5	0.2	2.2	69.4	3.6	0.7	0.0
22. Sumitomo Bank of California, San Francisco, CA	2392.0	101.3	4.2	1977.8	0.6	15.9	15.7	13.1	0.0	15.7
23. First Farmers Bank of Somerset Inc., Somerset, KY	127.4	3.0	2.4	83.8	3.6	3.4	112.9	2.3	0.0	0.0
*24. Heritage Bank, Anaheim, CA	190.2	5.2	2.7	125.0	3.3	20.1	387.4	16.1	0.0	56.0

Fifty Weakest Banks (With Assets Over $25 Million)

	Total Assets $ Mil.	Total Equity $ Mil.	Equity as % of Total Assets	Total Loans $ Mil.	Loan Loss Reserves as % of Total Loans	Loans 90 Days Past Due $ Mil.	% Equity	Non-Performing Loans $ Mil.	Renegotiated Loans $ Mil.	Brokered Deposits % Deposits
25. Bank of Oregon, Woodburn, OR	165.4	5.1	3.1	115.5	0.8	6.6	129.3	7.8	0.4	4.6
26. Girod Trust Company, San Juan, PR	354.9	18.9	5.3	165.9	0.6	16.6	87.4	11.0	0.8	0.0
*27. West Coast Bank, Los Angeles, CA	197.6	9.1	4.6	145.5	1.0	14.6	160.3	9.2	0.0	23.5
*28. Mississippi Bank, Jackson, MS	293.2	9.8	3.4	179.8	1.3	3.8	38.8	5.0	4.7	0.0
29. Bank Leumi & Trust Co. of New York	2533.1	92.4	3.7	1272.2	0.5	0.4	0.5	16.6	1.8	0.0
30. Daiwa Bank & Trust Co., New York, NY	929.7	39.2	4.2	318.2	0.8	0.0	0.0	2.2	0.0	0.0
31. Traders Nat'l Bank of Tullahoma, TN	30.4	0.9	3.1	16.9	5.2	0.4	45.8	1.6	0.8	0.0
32. First American Bank of Detroit, MI	1044.0	35.4	3.4	634.9	1.4	5.1	14.3	23.0	17.9	0.0
33. Manufacturers Hanover Trust Co., New York, NY	57001.5	2090.8	3.7	40238.7	0.8	126.9	6.1	350.9	118.3	0.0
34. First Pennsylvania Bank, Bala Cynwyd, PA	5123.1	196.8	3.8	2641.6	2.2	12.7	6.5	80.0	45.9	0.3

35. First National Bank of Chicago, IL	33751.9	1404.3	4.2	20983.7	1.0	17.5	1.2	527.5	67.3	2.8
36. Peoples Bank and Trust Co., Berea, KY	128.2	3.3	2.5	24.5	0.9	0.4	11.0	0.0	0.0	0.0
37. Independent State Bank of Minneapolis, MN	90.0	2.3	2.6	19.3	0.4	0.6	24.1	0.0	0.0	0.0
38. River Grove Bank & Trust Co., River Grove, IL	27.3	0.6	2.2	6.5	3.5	0.4	62.3	0.1	0.0	0.0
39. Citizens Bank of Weirton, WV	31.4	0.9	3.0	17.7	1.0	0.6	59.4	0.3	0.0	0.0
40. Commonwealth Bank, Torrance, CA	132.8	5.1	3.9	95.3	0.9	4.5	88.1	1.1	0.0	0.0
41. Bank America, San Francisco, CA	111707.9	4254.9	3.8	70388.9	0.9	0.0	0.0	0.0	0.0	0.6
42. City & County Bank of McMinn Cty., Athens, TN	28.0	0.8	2.9	14.8	1.1	0.2	18.2	0.7	0.0	1.1
43. European-American Bank & Trust, New York, N.Y.	6609.7	274.6	4.2	4244.4	0.8	60.8	22.1	96.8	11.4	0.0
44. Interfirst Bank of Dallas, TX	12004.3	419.2	3.5	6644.6	2.7	54.1	12.9	445.1	21.9	15.8
45. Bank of New England, Boston, MA	4660.4	168.1	3.6	2265.0	1.2	4.4	2.6	55.7	1.2	0.0
46. Adrian Buckhannon Bank, Buckhannon, WV	57.7	2.0	3.4	27.6	2.8	0.9	44.8	0.7	1.3	0.0
47. Continental Illinois Bank & Trust Co., Chicago, IL	39445.4	1809.6	4.6	29468.1	1.2	524.0	29.0	1561.0	218.3	1.4

Fifty Weakest Banks (With Assets Over $25 Million)

	Total Assets $ Mil.	Total Equity $ Mil.	Equity as % of Total Assets	Total Loans $ Mil.	Loan Loss Reserves as % of Total Loans	Loans 90 Days Past Due $ Mil.	% Equity	Non-Performing Loans $ Mil.	Renegotiated Loans $ Mil.	Brokered Deposits % Deposits
48. Bank of Beverly Hills, CA	87.1	4.0	4.6	56.1	1.9	2.3	56.2	2.3	0.8	0.9
49. Biscayne Bank, Miami, FL	95.0	7.9	8.3	56.0	1.2	0.9	126.4	8.2	1.2	0.6
*50. First Central Bank and Trust Co. of Del City, OK	130.5	8.5	6.6	90.0	0.9	7.5	88.0	11.6	0.7	27.2

Source: Federal Reserve Board Report of Condition, reproduced from The Holt Investment Advisory.
* Already closed subsequent to 9/30/83.

Fifty Strongest Banks (With Assets Over $25 Million)

	Total Assets $ Mil.	Total Equity $ Mil.	Equity as % of Total Assets	Total Loans $ Mil.	Loan Loss Reserves as % of Total Loans	Loans 90 Days Past Due $ Mil.	% Equity	Non-Performing Loans $ Mil.	Renegotiated Loans $ Mil.	Brokered Deposits % Deposits
1. Associates National Bank, Concord, CA	$51.3	$17.2	33.6%	$46.6	3.3%	0.5	2.7%	$0.1	$0.0	0.0%
2. First Blair City Nat'l Bank, Tyrone, PA	26.5	5.0	10.9	3.9	6.0	0.1	1.2	0.0	0.0	0.0
3. McDowell County Nat'l Bank, Welch, WV	80.3	15.9	19.8	15.1	3.9	0.3	1.6	0.0	0.0	0.0
4. First Wiscons n Trust Co., Milwaukee, WI	43.1	8.4	19.5	4.0	2.2	0.0	0.0	0.0	0.0	0.0
5. Citizens State Bank, Newport, IN	45.3	8.2	18.1	11.9	2.5	0.1	1.4	0.0	0.0	0.0
6. Farmers Bank & Capital Trust Co., Frankfort, KY	236.7	67.9	28.7	79.9	3.3	1.4	2.1	0.7	0.0	0.0
7. Bank of Harlan, Harlan, KY	32.5	6.5	20.1	13.6	2.1	0.0	0.4	0.3	0.0	0.0
8. First Nat'l Bank of Alliance	124.8	16.8	13.5	40.3	2.4	0.2	1.2	0.1	0.0	0.0
9. Citizens Bank, Colquitt, GA	28.7	6.1	21.2	6.6	2.7	0.0	0.7	0.2	0.0	0.0
10. Kentucky Farmers Bank of Catlettsburg, KY	76.8	11.7	15.2	30.3	3.4	1.6	14.0	0.1	0.0	0.0
11. Berwyn National Bank, Berwyn, IL	43.8	8.9	20.5	9.9	1.7	0.3	3.4	0.0	0.0	0.0

Fifty Strongest Banks (With Assets Over $25 Million)

	Total Assets $ Mil.	Total Equity $ Mil.	Equity as % of Total Assets	Total Loans $ Mil.	Loan Loss Reserves as % of Total Loans	Loans 90 Days Past Due $ Mil.	% Equity	Non-Performing Loans $ Mil.	Renegotiated Loans $ Mil.	Brokered Deposits % Deposits
12. Commercial Trust Company, Fayette, MO	32.9	6.3	19.1	10.9	1.7	0.6	10.2	0.0	0.0	0.0
13. Producers Bank & Trust Co., Bradford, PA	44.7	4.0	8.9	10.9	0.0	0.1	2.4	0.0	0.0	0.0
14. Bank of War, WV	25.2	3.8	15.3	4.7	1.7	0.1	2.9	0.0	0.0	0.0
15. Lawrenceburg Natl. Bank, Lawrenceburg, KY	35.4	4.6	13.1	11.2	2.7	0.3	5.5	0.1	0.0	0.0
16. Jefferson State Bank, San Antonio, TX	59.7	8.8	14.7	18.9	2.1	0.0	0.0	0.0	0.0	0.0
17. First National Bank of Blanchester, OH	25.4	3.7	14.6	6.3	1.8	0.1	1.5	0.0	0.0	0.0
18. Farmers and Merchants Bank, Des Arc, AR	25.2	4.7	18.8	6.5	1.6	0.0	0.1	0.0	0.0	0.0
19. Bank of Iaeger, WV	27.2	5.2	19.1	5.9	1.6	0.2	4.2	0.0	0.0	0.0
20. Citizens State Bank, Moundridge, KS	27.9	4.9	17.6	12.0	2.7	0.3	5.6	0.0	0.0	0.0
21. Western Greenbrier Natl. Bank, Rainelle, WV	29.0	5.4	18.5	2.1	1.4	0.0	0.1	0.0	0.0	0.0
22. Suburban Bank/ Delaware, Dover, DE	90.6	26.8	29.6	90.8	0.9	0.1	0.3	0.0	0.0	0.0
23. First Bank and Trust, Menomonie, WI	38.5	4.9	12.8	13.9	2.3	0.2	3.5	0.0	0.0	0.0

24.	District National Bank of Chicago, IL	54.9	7.4	13.5	8.2	3.1	0.2	3.1	0.0	0.0	0.0
25.	First Bank of Marietta, OH	27.5	3.9	14.2	14.5	2.7	0.5	12.0	0.0	0.0	0.0
26.	First National Bank in Donaldsonville, LA	40.0	5.2	13.0	13.3	2.8	0.2	4.1	0.0	0.0	0.0
27.	Putnam County National Bank of Carmel, NY	47.6	8.1	17.0	15.3	2.0	0.4	5.5	0.2	0.0	0.0
28.	Fulton State Bank, Fulton, IL	31.2	3.5	11.1	10.0	2.5	0.0	0.9	0.0	0.1	0.0
29.	Richardson County Bank & Trust Co., Falls City, NE	46.2	5.6	12.2	21.1	6.8	0.1	1.0	0.0	0.0	0.0
30.	Milwaukee County Bank, West Allis, WI	131.5	16.7	12.7	26.1	2.1	0.2	1.0	0.0	0.0	0.0
31.	First Trust and Savings Bank, Moville, IA	27.2	3.5	13.0	7.6	1.7	0.0	0.4	0.0	0.0	0.0
32.	Fairburn Banking Company, Fairburn, GA	29.5	3.7	12.5	11.2	2.3	0.6	16.0	0.0	0.0	0.0
33.	First National Bank of Mayfield, KY	40.3	7.9	19.7	11.1	1.3	0.0	0.5	0.0	0.1	0.0
34.	Farmers & Merchants Bank of Long Beach, CA	578.0	96.3	16.7	161.6	7.1	6.9	7.2	0.0	0.0	0.0
35.	First Omni Bank Nat'l Assoc., Millsboro, DE	110.0	25.8	23.5	100.3	1.7	0.2	0.7	0.0	0.0	0.0
36.	Iowa State Bank, Des Moines, IA	62.2	8.9	14.3	15.9	2.3	0.4	4.0	0.0	0.0	0.0
37.	First Clark National Bank of Northfork, WV	36.1	4.9	13.7	12.7	1.9	0.0	0.8	0.0	0.0	0.0

Fifty Strongest Banks (With Assets Over $25 Million)

	Total Assets $ Mil.	Total Equity $ Mil.	Equity as % of Total Assets	Total Loans $ Mil.	Loan Loss Reserves as % of Total Loans	Loans 90 Days Past Due		Non-Performing Loans $ Mil.	Renegotiated Loans $ Mil.	Brokered Deposits % Deposits
						$ Mil.	% Equity			
38. Indiana State Bank, Terre Haute, IN	89.8	13.0	14.5	28.4	1.6	0.1	0.6	0.0	0.0	0.0
39. Metairie Bank & Trust Co., Metairie, LA	129.2	18.5	14.3	55.7	1.5	0.7	3.8	0.0	0.0	0.0
40. Bank of Russell-ville, OH	27.7	3.6	12.9	4.5	1.9	0.0	1.1	0.0	0.0	0.0
41. Coconut Grove Bank, Miami, FL	126.0	13.7	10.9	25.3	3.1	1.0	7.0	0.1	0.0	0.0
42. Sun First Nat'l Bank of DeFuniak Springs, FL	32.0	4.1	12.8	6.9	1.9	0.0	0.9	0.1	0.0	0.0
43. Mid-American Bank and Trust of Louisville, KY	487.0	73.3	15.0	183.3	2.3	3.3	4.6	0.7	0.0	0.0
44. First Nat'l Bank of St. Charles, MO	98.7	12.9	13.1	42.1	2.1	0.2	1.7	0.6	0.0	0.0
45. Citizens Nat'l Bank of Hillsboro, TX	38.3	4.9	12.9	10.2	2.0	0.0	0.1	0.0	0.0	0.0
46. Bank of Neosho, MO	65.4	8.3	12.8	16.2	2.0	0.1	1.3	0.0	0.0	0.0
47. First National Bank of West Point, GA	51.7	6.4	12.4	20.1	2.0	0.1	2.0	0.1	0.0	0.0
48. McCook County National Bank, Salem, SD	28.7	3.9	13.5	16.6	5.1	0.0	0.0	0.5	0.4	0.0
49. Goodland State Bank & Trust Co., Goodland, KS	27.8	4.6	16.7	16.9	2.4	0.0	0.6	0.0	0.0	0.0
50. First State Bank, Elkhart, KS	30.1	3.2	10.5	6.3	4.1	0.1	2.2	0.0	0.0	0.0

Balance Sheet Totals of the World's Top One Hundred Banks

Bank	Headquarters	Balance Sheet Total (000's)
1 Citicorp	New York	$109,551,000
2 BankAmerica Corporation	San Francisco	$106,802,906
3 Caisse Nationale de Crédit Agricole	Paris	Frs.422,087,300
4 Banque Nationale de Paris	Paris	Frs.397,414,027
5 Crédit Lyonnais	Paris	Frs.446,327,645
6 Société Générale	Paris	Frs.410,027,000
7 Deutsche Bank	Frankfurt (Main)	DM.174,593,736
8 Barclays Bank Group	London	£37,097,000
9 National Westminster Bank Group	London	£34,569,000
10 Fuji Bank	Tokyo	Yen15,923,469,000
11 Sumitomo Bank	Osaka	Yen15,775,713,000
12 Chase Manhattan Corp.	New York	$72,997,772
13 Sanwa Bank	Osaka	Yen14,643,647,000
14 Dai-Ichi Kangyo Bank	Tokyo	Yen16,720,912,000
15 Dresdner Bank	Frankfurt (Main)	DM.123,105,545
16 Midland Bank Group	London	£25,342,700
17 Industrial Bank of Japan	Tokyo	Yen12,530,640,000
18 Mitsubishi Bank	Tokyo	Yen14,200,977,000
19 Mitsubishi Trust and Banking Corporation	Tokyo	Yen11,872,733,000
20 Westdeutsche Landesbank	Düsseldorf	DM.94,177,744
21 Manufacturers Hanover Corporation	New York	$53,415,308
22 Daiwa Bank	Osaka	Yen11,081,033,000
23 Cie. Financière de Paris et des Pays-Bas	Paris	Frs.237,754,000
24 Commerzbank Group	Düsseldorf	DM.100,028,926
25 Algemene Bank Nederland	Amsterdam	Fl.108,738,849
26 J. P. Morgan & Co. Incorporated	New York	$49,447,252
27 Banco do Brasil	Brasília	US$49,246,000
28 Royal Bank of Canada	Montreal	C$57,400,604
29 Mitsui Trust and Banking Co.	Tokyo	Yen10,284,591,000
30 Lloyds Bank Group	London	£19,866,000
31 Norinchukin Bank	Tokyo	Yen11,701,027,000

Balance Sheet Totals of the World's Top One Hundred Banks

Bank	Headquarters	Balance Sheet Total (000's)
32 Bayerische Vereinsbank	Munich	DM.91,504,640
33 National Bank of Abu Dhabi	Abu Dhabi	DH.17,387,954
34 Taiyo Kobe Bank	Kobe	Yen9,827,032,000
35 The Hongkong and Shanghai Banking Corporation	Hong Kong	HK$237,787,074
36 Centrale Rabobank	Utrecht	Fl.97,557,189
37 Bank of Tokyo	Tokyo	Yen11,080,823,000
38 Amsterdam-Rotterdam Bank (Amro Bank)	Amsterdam	Fl.94,294,376
39 Union Bank of Switzerland	Zurich	Frs.77,526,902
40 Canadian Imperial Bank of Commerce	Toronto	C$51,084,572
41 Bayerische Hypotheken- und Wechsel-Bank AG	Munich	DM.83,845,999
42 Swiss Bank Corporation	Basel	Frs.74,109,238
43 Tokai Bank	Nagova	Yen10,112,957,000
44 Continental Illinois Corp.	Chicago	$40,191,337
45 Banca Nazionale del Lavoro	Rome	L.32,219,710,000
46 Chemical New York Corp.	New York	$39,900,307
47 Mitsui Bank	Tokyo	Yen9,604,400,000
48 Sumitoma Trust and Banking Company	Osaka	Yen9,586,817,000
49 Banca Commerciale Italiana	Milan	L.35,446,671,000
50 Bayerische Landesbank Girozentrale	Munich	DM.74,534,682
51 Bank of Montreal	Montreal	C$43,926,112
52 Société Général de Banque	Brussels	Frs.1,164,205,000
53 Standard Chartered Bank	London	£15,416,900
54 Long Term Credit Bank of Japan	Tokyo	Yen8,993,716,000
55 Crédit Suisse	Zurich	Frs.63,475,080
56 Bank of Nova Scotia	Toronto	C$40,349,045
57 DG Bank (Deutsche Genossenschaftbank)	Frankfurt (Main)	DM.65,302,200
58 Bankers Trust New York Corporation	New York	$32,573,086

Balance Sheet Totals of the World's Top One Hundred Banks

	Bank	Headquarters	Balance Sheet Total (000's)
59	Western Bancorporation	Los Angeles	$31,062,284
60	Bank für Gemeinwirtschaft	Frankfurt (Main)	DM.60,379,305
61	Monte dei Paschi di Siena	Siena	L.27,532,600,000
62	Shoko Chukin Bank	Tokyo	Yen6,228,233,000
63	Instituto Bancario San Paolo di Torino	Turin	L.26,812,881,000
64	Crédit Industriel et Commercial	Paris	Frs.129,127,500
65	First Chicago Corporation	Chicago	$28,120,944
66	Yasuda Trust and Banking Company	Tokyo	Yen6,971,148,000
67	Credito Italiano	Milan	L.25,607,787,000
68	Cassa di Risparmio delle Provincie Lombarde	Milan	L.25,088,275,000
69	Security Pacific Corporation	Los Angeles	$26,673,745
70	Toyo Trust and Banking Co.	Tokyo	Yen6,578,950,000
71	Toronto Dominion Bank	Toronto	C$30,692,974
72	Banque Bruxelles Lambert	Brussels	Frs.739,739,328
73	Banco di Roma	Rome	L.23,434,809,000
74	Saitama Bank	Saitama	Yen5,270,459,000
75	Hessische Landesbank Girozentrale	Frankfurt (Main)	DM.48,145,603
76	Kyowa Bank	Tokyo	Yen6,130,707,000
77	Algemene Spaar en Lijfrentekas	Brussels	Frs.696,113,000
78	Norddeutsche Landesbank Girozentrale	Hannover	DM.40,138,000
79	Nippon Credit Bank	Tokyo	Yen5,746,627,000
80	Wells Fargo & Co.	San Francisco	$22,693,979
81	Nederlandsche Middenstandsbank	Amsterdam	Fl.47,865,578
82	Consorzio di Credito per le Opere Pubbliche	Rome	L.17,881,982,000
83	Hokkaido Takushoku Bank	Sapporo	Yen4,497,965,000
84	Crédit Communal de Belgique	Brussels	Frs.665,027,287

Balance Sheet Totals of the World's Top One Hundred Banks

Bank	Headquarters	Balance Sheet Total (000's)
85 Skandinaviska Enskilda Banken	Stockholm	Kr.90,175,000
86 Bank of Yokohama	Yokohama	Yen4,329,557,000
87 Kreditanstalt für Wiederaufbau	Frankfurt (Main)	DM.34,211,703
88 Commonwealth Banking Corporation	Sydney	A$17,049,079
89 Post-Och Kreditbanken, PK Banken	Stockholm	Kr.83,538,000
90 Banco di Napoli	Naples	L.17,755,484,000
91 Svenska Handelsbanken	Stockholm	Kr.82,906,000
92 Instituto Mobiliare Italiano	Rome	L.16,843,912,000
93 Banque de l'Indochine et de Suez (Indosuez)	Paris	Frs.84,810,460
94 Crocker National Corporation	San Francisco	$18,447,389
95 Bank of New South Wales	Sydney	A$15,401,622
96 Creditanstalt-Bankverein	Vienna	Sch.249,429,900
97 Irving Bank Corporation	New York	$17,530,896
98 Bank Melli Iran	Tehran	Rials1,250,699,111
99 Bank Leumi le Israel	Tel Aviv	IS.131,383,787
100 State Bank of India	Bombay	Rs.127,319,953

For the purpose of obtaining an accurate conversion into U.S. dollars or any other currency, daily rates should be consulted. The distortion in parities in recent years has already caused untold turmoil in world financial circles. With the exception of the first two banks, the balance of 98 were in entirely different positions in early 1984.

WITH WHOM SHOULD I DO BUSINESS?

Until a short while ago, I had a seemingly iron-clad formula: I would never recommend a broker or vendor who had been less than ten years in business; nor, unless I could speak from personal experience, would I recommend doing business with a banking institution less than a century old. However, the recent collapses of a prestigious London bullion house that was well over 100 years old and the fifth largest bank in the United States demolished my fashionable but arbitrary theory. Feeble U.S. and international financial institutions and shaky brokerage houses spell *caveat emptor.*

On balance, Canada's banking foundations are sounder than their American counterparts. As of April 1985, Canada has had only one near-collapse of a bank since the "dirty thirties"; 80 American financial institutions have folded in 1985 alone. That comes to almost one bankruptcy (and does not include shotgun marriages and forced mergers) per day. Illinois and Maryland have already declared forced bank holidays, and more states may follow.

As some anxiety about the U.S. situation may carry over to Canada, I have become cautious in recommending banking and trust facilities in Canada—and elsewhere. Regulatory controls make Canadian chartered banks my personal preference in North

America; also trust companies owned by chartered banks are usually sounder than the small privately-owned independents.

BROKERS

Australia
Rudolf Wolff & Co. Pty. Ltd.
80 Collins Street
Melbourne 3000
AUSTRALIA

– Commodity brokers

Canada
Alco Canada Commodities
  Services Inc.
800 Place Victoria, Suite 4708
P.O. Box 307
Montreal, Quebec
CANADA H4Z 1G8

– Commodity brokers with international facilities. Special department dealing, guiding and creating commodity trading clubs.

Orgold du Canada
International currency and
  bullion dealers
Main lobby, Montreal Stock
  Exchange
P.O. Box 678
Montreal, Quebec
CANADA H4Z 1J9
Tel: (514) 871-1717
24 hour information line:
  (514) 871-8444

United Kingdom
Rudolf Wolff & Co. Ltd.
2nd Floor, E Section
Plantation House
10–15 Mincing Lane
London EC3M 3DB
ENGLAND

– Commodity brokers

U.S.A.
Rudolf Wolff Inc.
295 Madison Avenue,
6th Floor
New York, New York
U.S.A. 10017

– Commodity brokers

Switzerland
Rudolf Wolff AG
Stadelhofer-Passage
Stadelhoferstrasse 18
CH–8024 Zurich
SWITZERLAND

– Commodity brokers

West Germany
Rudolf Wolff GMBH
Hohe Bleichen 20
2000 Hamburg 36
WEST GERMANY

– Commodity brokers

220

Montreal
Royal Bank
1 Place Ville Marie
Montreal, Quebec
CANADA H3C 3B9

Bank of Montreal
129 St. James St.
Montreal, Quebec
CANADA H2Y 1M6

National Bank of Canada
Public Relations
Tour de la Banque Nationale
600 de la Gauchetière W.
Montreal, Quebec
CANADA H3B 4L3

Toronto
Royal Bank
200 Bay Street
Toronto, Ontario
CANADA M5J 2J5

Bank of Montreal
First Bank Tower
First Canadian Place
Toronto, Ontario
CANADA M5X 1A1

Switzerland
Comexter S.A.
P.O. Box 63
Shêne Bougeries
1224 Geneva SWITZERLAND

– Personal and corporate portfolio management minimum US $ 100,000
or Suisse Francs 250,000

Special Updating Service
Klimm Management Corporation
P.O. Box 935
Tour de la Bourse
Montreal, Quebec
CANADA H4Z 1K2

Klimm Management will respond and forward limited updatings and market recommendations pertaining to strategies outlined in *Market Smarts*, free of charge. Please enclose a self-addressed, stamped envelope.

Daily Trading Signal

Readers already conversant with trading, or professional traders specializing in precious metals can write for more information to World Goldline, a daily trading signal service with an impressive record. Recently, the service has been extended to informing your broker, who has to report to account owners on each and every executed transaction. This service is highly professional. WGL is available for a trial period of one month for $75. Write P.O. Box 678, Tour de la Bourse, Montreal, Quebec, Canada H4Z 1J9, or telex 055–60329 (GOLD CORP.).

Newsletters/Strategy Information

In the chapter "Investment Newsletters," I introduced some critical comments about this once bubbling industry. Many hundreds of publications have come and gone in the last five years. Today we still have approximately 1,500 newsletters serving a particular clientele in North America.

The following short list should offer you a fair average of some publications that can claim long-term creditability. The editors are individuals who have gained extensive experience in their subject areas and may well be leaders rather than followers. I'm certain that even if you do not agree with everything you read in any one of these newsletters, the articles should encourage further research, which can only help you formulate a strategy for how to cope with the ensuing monetary rollover we are about to witness. Knowledge is power, and what you read in this book is to be supplemented with constant, updated information to enable you to stay ahead and, above all, take action to capitalize on what the future offers you.

Most of the listed publications will forward you a free copy of a past or current issue for evaluation. Most publications also have a special sampling rate.

* = ° ** *Barron's*—National Business & Financial Weekly, 22 Cortlandt St., New York, N.Y., U.S.A. 10007. Subscription: $76 U.S./year.

* ° + *Deliberations* by Ian McAvity, P.O. Box 182, Adelaide Street Station, Toronto, Ontario, M5G 2J1, Canada. Subscription: $215 Can. for 24 issues.

* ° *Dessauer's Journal of Financial Markets*, P.O. Box 1718, Oleans, MA, U.S.A. 02653. Published twice monthly. Subscription: $150 U.S./year.

** Newsletter *Digest* by Dr. Al Owen, 2335 Pansy Street, Huntsville, AL, U.S.A. 35801. Published 24 times a year. Subscription: $75 U.S./year.

+ * ° ▭ *Elliott Wave Theory* by Robert Prechter, New Classics Library, P.O. Box 1618, Gainsville, GA, U.S.A. 30503. Published monthly. Subscription: $100 U.S./year.

* ° ** *Holbach's Geldbrief* (money letter), Bahnhofstrasse 3, Postfach 58, CH–6312 Steinhaussen 2G. Published in German.

* ▭ ° *The Holt Investment Advisory*, 290 Post Road West, Wesport, CF, U.S.A. 06880. (Published first and third Friday of each month.) Subscription: $225 U.S./year.

° *Gold News Letter*, Editor J.U. Blanchard, 4425 W. Napoleon Ave., Metairie, LA, U.S.A. 70001. Published monthly. Subscription: $95 U.S./year.

* ° *The Granville Mark Letter Inc.*, P.O. Drawer 23006, Kansas City, MO, U.S.A. 64141. Published 46 times a year. Subscription: $250 U.S./year.

° ** *Myers Finance and Energy*, 642 Peyton Building, Spokane, WA, U.S.A. 99201. Published 14 times per year. Subscription: $200 U.S./year.

* Stocks; ▭ Bonds; ° Precious Metals; + Commodities; ** General, Digest.

For free information on trading commodity futures, write to:

Chicago Board of Trades
Marketing Department
LaSalle et. Jackson
Chicago, Illinois
U.S.A. 60604

For more specific information, write to:

Commodity Research Bureau Inc.
1 Liberty Plaza
New York, New York
U.S.A. 10006

GLOSSARY

Accommodation Paper: Bill of exchange or promissory note to which the acceptor, maker, drawer or endorser has added his guarantee for the purpose of assisting another party to obtain credit.

Acid Test: The fineness of gold determined through the exposure of the metal to nitric and hydrochloric acids.

Alloy: A mixture of metals. Gold is alloyed with silver, copper, zinc or other base metals to cause or obtain hardness or special color.

Arbitrageur: A trader who buys the same commodity in one market and simultaneously sells it on another market.

Assay: A test of metals in which purity is established. The assayer often carries out his analysis and marks the metal accordingly (*see* Fineness).

Bear: One who believes the trend of the market is down.

Broker: Any person who acts as an agent to establish contracts between two parties or acts as a dealer in the property of others.

Bull: One who believes the trend of the market is up.

Bullion Dealer: A firm or individual deriving major income through trading precious metals on the physical market.

Butterfly: A spread involving long positions in one month and short positions in another on the same exchange. Designed to reduce taxes; very unpopular with taxation authorities around the world.

Call: A commodity option or a stock option giving the holder the right to call away, from the account of the granter, a specific portion of a commodity at an agreed-upon price and date. The holder's risk is limited to the cost (premium plus commissions) of the call no matter how low the market moves during the lifespan of the option. The holder is not compelled to accept delivery of a commodity if the price upon delivery is unfavorable.

Car: A loose quantity term sometimes used to describe a contract, e.g., "a car of bellies." Derived from the fact that quantities of the product specified in a contract used to correspond closely to the capacity of a railroad car.

Cash Commodity: The actual physical commodity or financial instrument as distinguished from a futures commodity or financial instrument.

Cash Price or Spot Price: The price required for immediate settlement, as opposed to a transaction in futures where settlement is due some time in the future.

Cashier's Check: A check issued by a bank and signed by the cashier on behalf of the institute. The issuing bank is liable irrespective of the fact that it may have issued the check on behalf of a client or depositor. It is impossible to stop payment on a cashier's check under normal business circumstances.

Certificate of Deposit: A written acknowledgment of receipt of a sum of money on deposit with a financial institute to be repaid per terms indicated on the certificate.

Clearing House: A firm acting in a capacity to collect, remit or clear funds by check, promissory notes or wire transfer, mainly servicing member and associated firms.

Closing Range: The closing price (or price range) recorded during the period designated as the official close.

Commission (Roundturn): The one-time fee charged by a broker to a customer when a position is liquidated either by offset or delivery.

226

Corporation: A fictitious entity created through special laws and under special documents, which in most instances restricts and limits the liability of stockholders and owners to the amounts of money they have promised or contributed to the capital funding of the corporation.

Currency: Paper money presently exchangeable for paper used for calculating interest on accrued debt and serving as a useful medium for statistics.

CFTC: The Commodity Futures Trading Commission, an independent agency of the federal government, created by Congress in 1974 and activated in April 1975 for the purpose of regulating futures trading to protect customers.

Daily Trading Limit: The amount by which a contract in future commodities can be settled on an exchange higher than or lower than the previous day's settlement price.

Deposit: Money left with a bank or financial institution mixed among all other funds. Time deposit is usually exempt from audit.

Demand Deposit: A demand deposit can be called upon by a depositor via transfer instructions or the issuance of a check.

Equity: The amount of funds a trader in commodity futures would obtain if his account was liquidated at the settlement price.

Escheat: A concept relating to the title to property left unclaimed for a certain period, after which it is usually taken over by the government. Originates from English feudal laws—reversion of land to the lord or Crown.

Eurodollar: United States currency units held and traded outside the legal jurisdiction of the United States. Also Eurosterling, Euromarks, Euroyen.

Face Value: Pegged monetary value of a coin. Face value has to be divorced from intrinsic value, and particularly in gold coins it serves for identification and theoretical purposes only. The Canadian Maple Leaf coin had originally a face value of $50 but an intrinsic value of 1 ounce pure gold.

Fair Trade Laws: Laws of several U.S. states tolerating and enabling certain parties engaged in manufacturing of specified brands to establish and fix high prices without contravening cartel legislation.

Federal Deposit Insurance Corporation: A U.S. federal government agency established to insure accounts of depositors in member financial institutes to create stability and confidence among depositors.

Federal Reserve System: The U.S. equivalent of a central bank. Functions as a regulator for federally charted commercial banks. Also labeled as "The Bank of Bankers."

Fineness (fine gold/pure silver): A measurement expressed in thousand parts of an alloy. Pure gold is 1.000 or 24 karats. When gold is identified as 18 karats, it means that only .750 parts of fine gold are present in that particular alloy. Usually fine gold is expressed as .9999 pure and pure silver is identified as .999 fine.

Flat: Used mainly in the commodity futures market, in reference to traders showing neither holdings nor liabilities in their accounts.

Foreign Exchange: Currencies other than the domestic currency of the country where one domiciles.

Futures Account: An account at a registered commission house for the purpose of trading in commodity futures contracts.

Futures Contract: A contract between a buyer and seller of a commodity or security, setting its price and date of delivery. A gold buyer in the futures market undertakes to pay a certain amount for a specified quantity of gold deliverable or to be sold at a future date.

Futures Prices: Prices determined to be paid in the future for delivery of a commodity at a future date.

Gold Clause: A contract indexed to the price of gold for the purpose of calculations. Usually applied in an unstable economy where the prices of paper money fluctuate widely.

Gold Fix: Twice a day in the city of London at the offices of N. M.

Rothschild & Sons, five prominent London gold dealers meet and reach a consensus on the price of gold. Also referred to as the London Fix. The first fix takes place at 10:00 A.M., the second at 2:00 P.M. London time. The other four members are Johnson Matthey Bankers and Brokers, Sharps Pixley Ltd., Mocatta & Goldsmith and Samuel Montagu & Co. Ltd.

Gold/Silver Ratio: A yardstick dating back to biblical times, which referred to the number of ounces or units of silver needed to acquire one ounce or unit of gold. For many years the average ratio was approximately 16:1, namely, sixteen ounces of silver were needed to purchase one ounce of gold.

Gold Standard: A monetary system honoring the convertibility of all paper currency transactions into gold.

Guaranty: An agreement whereby a third party promises a creditor or lender to pay or make good the debt of a borrower in the event that the debtor fails to do so. U.S. domestic banks are barred from acting as guarantors but have in many instances contravened the law through the issuance of letters of credit.

Hallmark: A mark on precious metal bars denoting producer, a serial number and fineness of the metal.

Hedge: The purchase or sale of a futures contract as a temporary substitute for a merchandising transaction to be made at a later date. Usually it involves opposite positions in the cash market and the futures market at the same time.

Ingot: A silver bar weighing about 1,000 troy ounces. In the course of time the term has been applied to other metals as well.

Intrinsic Value: The actual fine precious metal content used in a fabricated coin or item of jewelry.

Investment Banking: The financing of long-term capital requirement for equity as distinguished from financing of working capital, generally the province of commercial banking.

Lawful Money: Anything deemed so and decreed by the regime in power.

Leverage: The ability to make an investment with a small down payment, as little as 10 percent or without paying in full for nominal value. Enables investors to utilize unemployed funds elsewhere.

Leverage Contracts: Contracts with limited risk, by and large substitutes for options.

Libel: A defamatory written statement which may cause damage to the defamed party. A bank handing out untrue credit information may be liable for damages.

Limit Move: The maximum price or yield move up or down from the previous session's settlement price for a given contract allowed by exchange rules for any one day's trading.

London Delivery Bar: A gold bar weighing about 400 troy ounces of .995 minimum fineness. It bears markings of an assayer or refiner, usually recognized and accepted internationally.

London Gold Market: London is one of the world's leading gold centers. Two daily gold fixings establish the price of the metal, denominated in terms of U.S. dollars (*see also* Gold Fix).

Long: One who has bought a futures contract to establish a market position, and who has not yet closed out this position through an offsetting sale or by taking delivery.

Maintenance Margin: After paying in the initial margin required to trade, the equity position of an account according to market movements. An account short in gold in a rising market will require more cash to maintain the position. Known also as maintenance or variation margin. In the same fashion, if an account is long in a declining market, the maintenance of minimum cash will be required to keep an account operational by the end of each trading day.

Margin (Initial): A cash amount of funds that must be deposited with the broker for each futures contract as a guarantee of fulfilment of the futures contract. It is not considered as part payment of purchase. Also called Security Deposit.

Maximum Fluctuation: (*see* Limit Move)

Minimum Fluctuation: Smallest increment of price or yield movement possible in trading a given contract. For example, the minimum price fluctuation on one pork belly contract is 2½/100¢ per pound, or $9.50 per contract.

Money: Store of value, anything used as a medium of exchange. Throughout history, money in the first place was gold or silver. Currently used paper moneys answer only in part to the main functions expected of money. Paper notes are a medium of exchange at fluctuating rates; however, they do not qualify to the main function "Stores of Values."

Movement or Velocity: Representing the change calculated by dividing current prices by earlier prices over a specific period.

Negotiability: A note payable to a name, person or party becomes negotiable if it incorporates after the party's name or parties' names, "or order or bearer."

Offshore Banking: Banks established outside one's country of domicile. Often referred to as located in tax havens such as Jersey Island, Caribbean, West Indies, Liechtenstein, etc.

Open Interest: Number of open contracts. Refers to unliquidated purchases or sales but never to their combined total.

Opening Price: The price (or range) recorded during the period designated by the exchange as the official opening.

Option: The right to purchase or sell a commodity or security at a specified time in the future.

Overdraft: The issuance of a payment instruction in an amount exceeding the balance payable in an account.

Paper Trading: Trading futures or stocks where no real cash is employed. Often used by business schools, recommended for beginner traders to acquire transaction discipline and making business decisions.

Point: (*see* Minimum Fluctuation)

Position: An interest in the market, either long or short, in the form of open contracts.

Premium: The difference between cash and the future price of a commodity or security; in gold coins it refers to the amount over and above intrinsic (meltdown) value. A Krugerrand or

Maple Leaf may command a price of 2 percent to 3 percent over fine gold content.

Private Banks: A bank which does not publish its financial statements. The owners accept unlimited liability to the depositors and creditors. Private banks may specify introductions, minimum balances prior to accepting new accounts.

Public Outcry: The method used to buy and sell commodity futures in certain trading pits.

Safety Deposit Service: Facilities available for hire by many banks for the purpose of storage of valuables. Unless specified, safety deposit boxes are insured for nominal amounts only and rentees must make their own insurance arrangements in most instances.

Short: One who has sold a futures contract to establish a market position and who has not yet closed out this position through an offsetting purchase or by making delivery. The opposite of being long.

Silver Fix: Each trading day after the morning gold fix, three out of five London gold merchants assemble at Mocatta & Goldsmith to establish the silver price of that day. The three are: Johnson Matthey Bankers and Brokers, Mocatta & Goldsmith and Samuel Montagu & Co. Ltd. There is only one silver fixing (morning) in London.

Speculator: One who attempts to anticipate price changes and through market activities make profits; he is not using the futures market in connection with the production, processing, marketing or handling of a product.

Spread: A market position that is simultaneously long and short equivalent amounts of the same contract in different months or related contracts in the same or different months.

Stop Loss: A buying or selling order placed against an existing contract. A stop loss is designed to minimize potential loss insofar as if prices reach the nominated level, the order is automatically activated.

Stop Payment: An order issued by the drawer of a check to his bank reversing an order to pay. A bank may be held liable if it fails to carry out the order.

Switch: A procedure where the holder of a commodity futures contract in a certain month of delivery offsets his position simultaneously, switching to another month.

Tax Avoidance: Legal means to minimize payments of tax.

Tax Evasion: Illegal means to minimize payment of taxes. The interpretation of avoidance versus evasion varies from one country to another.

Tax Haven: A country or a jurisdiction where only minimal or no taxes on income, capital gains, transfer upon death and interest are being levied.

Technical Rally or Decline: A price movement resulting from conditions developing within the futures market itself and not dependent on outside supply and demand factors. These conditions include changes in the open interest, volume and degree of recent price movement.

Tick: Refers to a minimum change in price or yield, either up or down (*see also* Minimum Fluctuation).

Trading Limits: The amount of commodity futures contracts can carry in terms of settling the price of the previous day.

Trust Company: An institute authorized to hold property for the benefit of other parties on a trustee basis. Trust companies engage in mortgages and some jurisdictions may provide limited banking services.

Usuary: Interest levied on loans in excess of the highest rate permitted by law.

Volume: The number of futures contracts traded during a specified period of time.

Whipsaw Losses: Short-term market movements adversely affect trading positions. Buying (going long) in a declining market or selling (going short) in a short-term rising market. The term applies to traders who swiftly reverse from long to short or vice versa to be losing on both transactions. A whipsaw market is a rather untrending and erratic one.

INDEX

234

Stock market, 147-151, 152-157, 185
Stocks, *see* Shares.
Stop-loss points, 129
Strategic metals, 160-166
Survival needs, 83-85, 86
Sweden, 117, 152-153
Swing traders, 123-139
Swiss banks, 30, 41-47, 61, 85, 86,
    95-96
    choosing, 43-44

Tax evasion, 115-120
Tax havens, 45-47, 118, 176
Tax revolt, 118, 119-120
Technology, 15-16
Texaco, 72
Thailand, 116-117
Thatcher, Margaret, 156
Theft, 21-22
Third World, 13, 143, 179
    borrowers of Eurodollars, 32-34,
        36-38
    debtor nations, 35, 49-50, 59-60,
        61, 67-70, 73, 74
    gold holdings, 101-102
    and oil prices, 65, 73
Titanium, 163, 164-165
Totalitarianism, 12
Trade agreements, 58
Transaction costs, 129

Turkey, 34

Underground economy, 115-120
    in diamonds, 168
    government intervention in,
        118-119
Unemployment, 58, 155-156
United American Bank, Knoxville,
    22-23
United States
    dollar, 53-55, 57, 58, 68, 75, 85, 86,
        95, 139
    grain sales to U.S.S.R., 55-56, 57
    growth and decay of, 10-12
    and oil companies, 71-72
    policy on natural gas pipeline, 56
    underground economy in, 117-119

Vietnam War, 58

"Wall Street Week," 123
Warehouse receipts, 105-106
Wars, 7, 87
    real wealth during war and politi-
        cal instability, 85, 86, 87, 90
West Germany, 116, 153
Windfall profits tax, 71
World Goldline, 222

Zaire, 143, 165, 170, 180